I0121689

The English Local Government System

First Published in 1946, *The English Local Government System* has undoubtedly been one of the most successful introductory books on this subject. The purpose of this book is not so much to describe the various local government services, but rather to discuss the machinery and methods utilized in the provision of these services.

It discusses crucial themes like business yardsticks; the constitutional setting; judicial control; the associations of local authorities; the financial basis; state grants and providing for capital expenditure; the local authority's constitution; the impact of politics on administration; delegation of powers to committees; the need for reform; and central local relationships. This is an important historical reference work for students of public administration and British government and politics.

The English Local Government System

J. H. Warren

Routledge
Taylor & Francis Group

First published in 1946
by George Allen & Unwin Ltd

This edition first published in 2024 by Routledge
4 Park Square, Milton Park, Abingdon, Oxon, OX14 4RN

and by Routledge
605 Third Avenue, New York, NY 10017

Routledge is an imprint of the Taylor & Francis Group, an informa business

© This Eighth Revised Edition George Allen & Unwin Ltd., 1965

Publisher's Note
The publisher has gone to great lengths to ensure the quality of this reprint but points out that some imperfections in the original copies may be apparent.

Disclaimer
The publisher has made every effort to trace copyright holders and welcomes correspondence from those they have been unable to contact.

A Library of Congress record exists under LCCN: 66050420

ISBN: 978-1-032-90292-0 (hbk)
ISBN: 978-1-003-54694-8 (ebk)
ISBN: 978-1-032-90293-7 (pbk)

Book DOI 10.4324/9781003546948

THE ENGLISH
LOCAL GOVERNMENT
SYSTEM

by

J. H. WARREN
M.A., D.P.A., Solicitor

*formerly General Secretary, National and
Local Government Officers' Association
Sometime Town Clerk, Slough
Sometime External Lecturer in Public
Administration for Liverpool University*

Revised by

PETER G. RICHARDS
B.SC. (Econ), PH.D.
Reader in Politics, University of Southampton

GEORGE ALLEN & UNWIN LTD
MUSEUM STREET · LONDON

FIRST PUBLISHED IN MARCH 1946
SECOND IMPRESSION OCTOBER 1946
THIRD IMPRESSION 1947
REVISED SECOND EDITION (FOURTH IMPRESSION) 1949
THIRD EDITION, REVISED, RESET, AND ENLARGED (FIFTH IMPRESSION) 1953
FOURTH EDITION (SIXTH IMPRESSION) 1955
FIFTH EDITION (SEVENTH IMPRESSION) 1957
EIGHTH IMPRESSION 1959
SIXTH EDITION REVISED, AND ENLARGED 1961
SEVENTH EDITION (TENTH IMPRESSION) 1963
EIGHTH EDITION, REVISED AND RESET (ELEVENTH IMPRESSION) 1965

GERMAN TRANSLATION : 'SELBSTVERWALTUNG
IN ENGLAND' (WOLFGANG METZNER, FRANKFURT, 1952)
HINDI TRANSLATION : NOVELTY BOOK CO. PATNA

Printed in Great Britain
by East Midland Printing Co Ltd
Bury St. Edmunds, Suffolk

PREFATORY NOTE

Mr. Warren was able to revise his well-known book at the end of 1959, but after his death in 1960 further revisions bringing the book up-to-date have been carried out by Dr. Peter G. Richards, Reader in Politics at the University of Southampton, who has now undertaken the General Editorship of the *Town and County Hall Series* in succession to Mr. Warren.

INTRODUCTION TO THE EIGHTH EDITION

THE FOLLOWING pages aim to provide a concise but comprehensive account of the local government system of England and Wales. Their purpose is not so much to describe the various local government services, many of which are dealt with in other more specialised volumes in this series. Rather is the intention to discuss the machinery and methods utilised in the provision of these services. It will be necessary to outline the legal principles which control our local administration, for these have a profound influence on what it does and the way in which it works. Nevertheless, the main concern is to discuss the machinery of local government and the procedure of local authorities in order to promote an understanding of their administrative problems.

There are several classes of reader whose needs have been kept in mind in the preparation of this work. It will, it is hoped, answer the kind of questions asked by those with a social conscience that prompts the need to learn something of public life and activity. It will give the student of the social sciences, or the social worker, an inside picture of an institutional structure they usually see only from the outside. In particular, it is designed to meet the needs of young local government officers preparing for examinations or who desire to enlarge their background knowledge. And finally it is designed to give elected members of local authorities a fuller understanding of the system within which they work, of principles and procedure that experience has shown to be best and of certain broad questions that they themselves are called upon to decide for their own local councils.

The book is not designed primarily as a contribution to local government controversy, but no attempt has been made to avoid the expression of personal opinions on topics where there are widespread differences of view. Factual material devoid of any thread of argument is dull and lifeless, and it is hoped that the more controversial passages may stimulate discussion. As I have added some ideas to those originally propounded by Mr. Warren, it is now appropriate that I should accept responsibility for the opinions expressed in the book.

The English Local Government System has undoubtedly been one of the most successful introductory books on this subject. Nearly twenty years have passed since it first appeared, and in this time many alterations have occurred in the problems facing local authorities. Some issues and some experience that were important in 1946 are less so today: fresh questions have emerged in a contemporary Britain where the pace of change is rapid. Thus in the Eighth Edition note is taken of the latest developments, e.g. the important London Government Act, 1963, and a number of other adjustments have been made. There is much fuller treatment of the influence of party politics on local councils and some mention is made of the work of local authority associations. The reorganisation of local government structure is now given a separate chapter and the final chapter 'Problems of Today and Tomorrow' has been somewhat changed. But the book still retains the fruits of Mr. Warren's experience and judgment to which it is unnecessary for me to pay tribute.

I am much indebted to Miss D. Marshallsay, B.A.,A.L.A., Librarian of the Ford Collection of Parliamentary Papers, who has prepared the Index for this edition.

PETER G. RICHARDS

University of Southampton.
1964.

CONTENTS

CHAPTER I

The Services—Their Range and Character

FEW PEOPLE OUTSIDE the Local Government Service, or the circles interested in politics and government, realize the enormous range of local government today. There is no section of the community which it does not serve in some way. To some sections of the community it ministers continuously, from the cradle to the grave. Particularly is this true of the working classes, and these make up the bulk of our populace.

Let us illustrate the situation by following the successive phases of an average citizen's life and seeing how Local Government ministers to him in them all. It begins to do so before he is born, his pre-natal welfare, and the care of his mother, being the concern of the Local Authority's Maternity and Child Welfare Service. At birth, both mother and child may be cared for by its Midwifery Service. For two years after birth the child continues to have some measure of help, at post-natal clinics, from the Maternity and Child Welfare Service. In the succeeding three years, and before the child attains the age for scholastic education, he may attend a Nursery School associated with the Education Service. At five years of age he passes into the care of the Local Authority's Education Service for scholastic education and may so remain until he leaves school at the age of 15: he may, of course, stay on at school until 18 or continue his education at a technical college provided by the local education authority. With the aid of a local authority grant he may gain admission to a university. During the first school years the Education Service may, in circumstances of necessity, provide him with clothes and boots, and it will extend to him, as a matter of course, school meals, medical examination, and a measure of medical care. At school, he will be provided with recreational facilities in gymnasia, baths, or playing fields attached to the school, apart from any use he may make of similar facilities provided by the Local Authority for the general public in parks, recreation grounds, and open spaces.

Special help and protection will be given to him if he is blind, deaf, dumb, or lacking proper parental care.

When the child passes into employment, the Local Authority will still continue to extend the help of its Education and Welfare Services. These may continue to furnish him with technical instruction or cultural education in Technical Colleges, Evening Institutes, or classes run by voluntary bodies such as the Workers' Educational Association with the Local Authority's help; with the facilities of Youth Clubs; and with continuing help and protection if he is under such disabilities as were mentioned in the last paragraph.

During all this time the parental home may be a Council house provided by the Local Authority under the Housing Acts; and whether this be so or not, the home will be provided with at least one service by the Local Authority, namely sewerage, and it is more than likely that the Local Authority will also be supplying it with water. When the child grows up and marries it may again be the Local Authority which provides him with a dwelling-house, and the services mentioned.

Day by day, throughout his life, the citizen will move in and among streets, houses, shops, factories, offices, churches, schools, and places of amusement, the building of which has been regulated by the Local Authority under the Public Health code and the by-laws relating to new streets and buildings, and either in accordance with modern planning ideals, or at least in a conscious desire to mitigate the ugly congestion and squalor left behind by the early industrial age. In his passage along the streets he will often be conveyed by the municipality's buses.

All this aggregate of 'building development', as it is called, will be protected, as also will the lives and property of the citizens at large, by the Local Authority's police, fire, and ambulance services; and will be maintained in a sanitary condition by its street cleansing and refuse-removal services, its sewerage system, and its plants for sewage disposal, refuse-destruction, and the recovery of salvage.

Services such as these last mentioned are obviously the basic and indispensible ones for civilized life in any modern urban community; but the Local Authority does not stop short at communal provision of this kind but also acts as an agent of mental and aesthetic culture. In almost any city or large town in England our citizen may find his tastes and interests catered

THE SERVICES — THEIR RANGE AND CHARACTER

for by a municipal art gallery, museum, and reference library; and lending libraries will be available for him whether he lives in town or country.

When he goes on holiday to the seaside he finds the municipality catering for his lighter amusement in forms too innumerable to describe.

Finally, as the average citizen enters his declining years, illness and want may call once more for the Local Authority's succour through its welfare services; and whether this be so or not, and whether he die young or old, he will, more likely than not, be interred in the municipal cemetery, or cremated in a municipal crematorium.

Many of the municipality's normal services are hardly noticed by those most benefited, and it is usually the indispensable services, such as sewerage and the supply of water, that go most unnoticed. It is not easy for the housewife, as she turns on the tap or empties the sink, to appreciate the organization and engineering skill that have enabled such vital needs to be satisfied by such simple operations, or the vigilance and foresight that are necessary if services of this kind are to be at all times available, no matter how a locality may grow.

As may be expected, a range of services as wide and varied as we have indicated is reflected in an extraordinary variety of professions and occupations. All aspects of the municipality's work call for the services of administrators, lawyers, accountants, architects, civil engineers, and surveyors. The public health, education, and maternity and child welfare services employ a variety of medical and nursing staff. The public health services call in some places for the services of analysts and laboratory assistants. Cemeteries, mortuaries, and crematoria require superintendents or managers. The sanitary services, such as sewerage and water supply, employ engineers, industrial chemists, and several varieties of technician. The education services employ every kind of school-teacher, primary, secondary, technical, or commercial, not to speak of instructors, in art, music, and handicrafts, and teachers in physical training. The various 'protective' services employ police officers, coroners, fire brigade officers, public health inspectors, and weights and measures inspectors. The 'trading' or 'public-utility' undertakings employ water engineers, mechanical engineers, transport managers, and in some places tunnel managers, aerodrome managers, bridge managers, harbour and dock managers, and ferries managers (with various grades of ships' officers and engineers). The cultural activities engage the services of librarians, curators of museums, curators of art galleries (and in some places scientists and experts in applied art), organists, orchestral conductors, musicians, and bandsmen. The recreational services employ entertainment managers, restaurant managers, horticulturists, landscape-gardeners, professional golfers, golf-course managers, and swimming instructors. Nor are there wanting one or two odd professions and occupations such as rat-catchers, water-diviners, oyster-bed cultivators, and race-course managers. All the occupations cited are of 'staff' grade: the manual workers engaged also represent a wide variety of occupations and are of course more numerous.

BUSINESS YARDSTICKS

There is yet one more angle from which the range of municipal administration may be assessed, i.e. the business angle. This is best measured by the capital engaged, and the annual turnover.

In 1961-2 the outstanding capital debt of the Local Authorities as a whole amounted to £6,460 million. This figure, though the most useful figure available for our purpose, considerably understates the magnitude of the Local Authorities' capital assets when compared with the called-up capital of a company. It represents the residue of an aggregate loan capital of which much has been paid off through Sinking Funds, and not all of this for wasting assets which require periodical renewal. The Local Authorities own a considerable amount of property, particularly real estate, which is debt-free and not reflected in the figure given above. Even so, this figure of £6,460 million is sufficiently impressive. £544 million of it represented outlay on 'trading' enterprises, i.e. those productive of a monetary income which ordinarily obviates any charge to the rates for these services, and on estates from which some income is derived.

The annual turnover is best gauged by the aggregate expenditure, and this, in the same year 1961-2 amounted to £2,964 million of which £741 million was spent on capital works.

Annual revenue amounted to £2,268 million. This comprised in round figures £747 million rate-revenue; £830 million representing the total of grants made to Local Authorities by the State for services which the Local Authorities conduct but which the State partly pays for; and £690 million from trading undertakings, estates and minor sources.

As will appear more fully from Chapter II, the number of Local Authorities is quite large, and there are great differences among them in area, population, and range of function. It is not possible, therefore, to pass them all under review here, in assessing the scale of their activities on an individual footing. The data following will serve, however, to illustrate the scale to which administration can go in a single unit of the system.

The Birmingham City Council, administering the largest of English cities, with a population in 1963 of 1,115,630, had a net outstanding debt at 31st March 1963 of £188 million. In 1962-3 its revenue expenditure amounted to £68 million. Its permanent employees in all categories number about 50,000. Other towns, although smaller, produce figures with a similar *per capita* basis. In County Councils the scale of activity is necessarily lower because the tasks of local government are shared between the Counties and smaller authorities; in particular, the Counties are not primarily responsible for housing nor do they operate trading services. Thus Lancashire, the largest county in terms of population, has almost exactly twice as many inhabitants as Birmingham, but its net debt in 1963 amounted to £49 million, its capital expenditure in 1962-3 was £9 million and its current expenditure came to £73 million. *Per capita* these are well below the comparable Birmingham statistics.

Figures such as these make it obvious that the scale of business of our largest local authorities is comparable with that of the giant units in industry; and it could be demonstrated that the component services which make up their overall task present much more variety and contrast.

The total manpower engaged in Local Government in England and Wales was estimated by the Ministry of Labour to be nearly 1,700,000 in June, 1963. This figure included 426,000 part-time workers, many of whom are women employed in catering (including school canteens), school cleaning, in day nurseries and homes for children and aged persons.

B

HOW THE SERVICES ORIGINATED

The social and financial policies which govern the conduct of the services, collectively or individually, can hardly be understood without a full knowledge of the historical background. Concerned as we are more with administration than policy, we cannot detail the history of the services here. But a bare outline is essential to an understanding of the wide differences which exist between one service and another, and which the administrative organization of the Local Authority must accommodate.

For the most part the services are comparatively new, having originated in the early part of the nineteenth century; and it needs little imagination to realize that they are almost entirely a product of the Industrial Revolution. There are a few amenities, such as markets, and even water supply in its more primitive forms, which the Local Authorities of today inherited from the ancient chartered corporations of the medieval gild system; but in general the Industrial Revolution called for new services, in order to meet the new ways of living brought about by a mechanical age.

There were two broadly contrasted lines of social impulse along which the early industrial age forced the upgrowth of Local Authority services.

In the first place, an industrial civilization had then, as it has now, certain positive and indispensable requirements of its own in the matter of public services. To put it at the least, even production by competitive private enterprise cannot proceed far unless the State is fulfilling its minimum essential functions of protecting life and property; and even the most extreme theories of *laisser-faire* recognized the need for what political theory calls the police functions of the State. It was eventually recognized however that the requirements of the prevailing mode of production went even further than this, calling for such urban amenities as streets and public lighting as contributory to the efficiency of production if not a condition precedent to it. And when the new industrialism led to the creation of towns of greater size than ever before, many of them new, painful experience enforced a recognition that sanitary services of a communal nature are a first essential in such places, if humanity, whether rich or poor, is to survive at all in them. After the first onset of industrialism a movement sets in, therefore, for the provision of adequate facilities for the maintenance of industry and the town life associated with it.

The second impetus to the establishment of municipal services was the reaction against the social evils of early industrialism and in particular against the consequences of the economic doctrine of *laisser-faire* preached by the early classical economists such as Adam Smith and Ricardo. This reaction, arising after the 'forties, sustained throughout the remainder of the nineteenth century, and still continuing in this century, has given us what we now call our Social Services, some in the hands of the State, others in the hands of the Local Authorities. In many instances the initiative which led to the establishment of such services proceeded from the Local Authorities, and theirs was the experimental work, carried out under developments of the Poor Law, or under Local Private Acts which the Local Authorities themselves promoted. Parliament later adopted most of these experiments, and the Social Services as they exist today embody social measures of national scope with objects going far beyond any purely local concern. Those which the Local Authorities provide they conduct from a political standpoint, as agents of the State, though, legally, as principals.

The reaction against *laisser-faire* also established one further characteristic group of Local Authority services, namely the Trading Services as they are called—the supply of water, street transport, and until recently gas and electricity. Whether in private or company hands, undertakings in this sphere belong to that class of economic undertaking to which we attach the term 'public utility'—a term meaningless in itself but implying a service taken outside the prevailing sphere of free private enterprise and subjected in some measure or manner to organized community control. Largely through the agitation of the Local Authorities and the pressure they exerted upon Parliament on behalf of the consumers they represented, the reaction led firstly to a profound modification of the form taken by private enterprise in the conduct of these services, and secondly in many areas, to the supersession of private by municipal provision. Public-utility undertakings of the kind we speak of usually take the form of local regulated monopolies. If in municipal hands, they are subject to some statutory and central administrative control over prices and capitalization; and if in company hands, they have in some instances been further subjected to limitations of profit, and to provisions which prevent watering of capital to evade such limitations.

The history of these services begins with the first attempts to supply the new towns of the Industrial Revolution with gas and water. In conformity with the prevailing theory of economic *laisser-faire* the field was left open to private enterprise, and competing companies often laid three or four mains in the same street. This was so palpably wasteful as to bring about a recognition that the general economic doctrine could not apply in this sphere. Prices might, indeed, through such a competition, 'fluctuate at a level very little above cost', to use the phrase of the classical economists; but it was evident that they would fluctuate at a level of cost much higher than it need be. Competition in such circumstances could in any event not last, since an industry in which so high a proportion of capital is required for fixed distributive plant must possess a specially rapid tendency to monopoly. Competition soon gave way to amalgamation and local monopoly; and the last phases in the history of these services are those in which the consumers, through the Local Authorities, forced Parliament to regulate the monopolies and often secured powers by Private Act to buy out the companies and run the services themselves. When electricity supply and street transport arose in the 'seventies and 'eighties, Parliament recognized that these services had the same characteristics and tendency to monopoly as gas and water supply, and provided in advance that they should be carried on either as regulated private monopolies or as public monopolies undertaken by the Local Authorities. Under postwar nationalization measures, both municipal and company gas and electricity undertakings have been integrated under State ownership and operation. The range of Local Authority trading services is now therefore considerably narrower than it was. Water-supply and local passenger road transport services, i.e. 'trams and buses' are still however a fairly common feature in the field; and there is a variety of undertakings peculiar to particular places, e.g. tunnels, bridges, and docks, which also fall within it.

THE STAGES OF DEVELOPMENT

Let us now trace the broad phases in the upgrowth of the services.

Local Government begins with a nucleus of police and regulative powers. After the first of the modern organs of local government, i.e. the reformed Municipal Boroughs, had been set up in the older towns by the Municipal Corporations Act of 1835, the chief duty of their new democratically elected Borough Councils was to administer, through Watch Committees, the new Police Forces of which the first had been set up in the Metropolis in 1829. It may be objected that the oldest local government service of all, namely the Poor Law, which originated in the reign of Elizabeth, rather belies the suggestion that the earliest services were those in the sphere of police or regulative powers. Only remnants of it remain with the Local Authorities today, on a new footing, as part of the newer social services; but originally it was as much a measure of discipline as of social help. Indeed, the struggle to humanize it after the 'new' Poor Law of 1834 was a prominent feature of that later phase of municipal development which yielded the social services.

The first expansion of services came about with the struggle for town sanitation, led by Edwin Chadwick and John Simon; the first substantial legislative measures being the various Town 'Clauses' Acts of 1847, and the Public Health Act of 1848, the latter being the outcome of the Report of the Royal Commission on the Health of Towns in 1845, one of the major social documents of the nineteenth century. These measures fell far short of a satisfactory regulation of sanitary conditions, and a Sanitary Commission of 1869 had to give renewed attention to the subject before legislation on the subject became effective. A series of measures was passed in the next few years; and was eventually crowned by the great Public Health Act of 1875, which has since been consolidated, after further measures of 1890, 1907 and 1925, in the Public Health Act of 1936, the major code still current.

Accompanying the struggle for town sanitation was the struggle for public education, a service which, judged by its mixture of motives, is partly a communal and partly a social service. As is well known, education for the working classes was first provided by voluntary agencies, notably those of the Churches, the pioneers being Joseph Lancaster, a Quaker and in educational matters a 'non-sectarian', and Andrew Bell, a Churchman who upheld the principle of religious influence in popular education. The British and Foreign Society was formed in 1808 to provide schools on Lancaster's principles, and the National Society in 1811 to provide schools on Bell's, both societies being at first sustained by voluntary contributions. The voluntary system struck deep root; and throughout most of the century public education policy resolved itself into an expansion of the aid given, and an elaboration of the conditions upon which it was given, to the two pioneer voluntary societies and to those subsequently established by other religious bodies. A Royal Commission appointed in 1858 reported that 75 per cent of the scholars at the voluntary schools attended Church of England Schools; 10 per cent those of the British and Foreign Society; 5½ per cent those of the Roman Catholic Church; 4 per cent those of the Wesleyan Methodists; and 2 per cent those of the Congregationalists. Not until 1870, after an agitation which, in its culminating phases, was led by Chamberlain and his caucus of Birmingham Radicals, did State educational policy include the provision of rate-aided schools provided by Local Authorities (then the School Boards). The voluntary system was also retained, however, and the Balfour Education Act of 1902 provided that the voluntary schools also should be given a measure of rate aid. The voluntary system was in fact retained, though with many changes, by the major Education Act of 1944. The Act of 1902 brought the Local Authorities into the sphere of secondary education.

Apart from education, the movements of social conscience and working-class pressure which brought about the social services were of much later origin, and most of these services are a product of the present century. There was a trivial beginning with housing by the passing of the Housing of Working Classes Act in 1890, but it was not until after the war of 1914-1918 when, for a variety of reasons, an acute shortage of working-class and lower-middle-class housing accommodation had accrued, that municipal housing established itself, and was dealt with, through many fluctuations of policy, by the Addison Act of 1919, the Chamberlain Act of 1923, the Wheatley

Act of 1924, the Greenwood Act of 1930, and the Young Act of 1935, all now consolidated in the Housing Act of 1958.

Those medical services in which the individual's welfare rather than the protection of the community is the dominant motive, and which are therefore to be thought of as social rather than protective services, also fell well within the present century. Control over infectious diseases, which can be regarded as part of protective and sanitary legislation, was dealt with by the Act of 1875 and subsequent Acts of 1889 and 1890; though the treatment of tuberculosis did not originate until 1915, and of venereal diseases until 1918. The school-meals service did not originate until 1906, school medical inspection until 1907, and maternity and child welfare until 1918, if we except the tentative approach to this latter service which was made by the Notification of Births Act, 1915.

The municipalization of gas, water, electricity, and street transport was a feature of the latter part of the nineteenth century. In two spheres—gas and water—the municipal services were for the most part established in supersession of private enterprises under Local Private Acts promoted by the Local Authority. Electricity was in many areas, and tramway transport in most areas, pioneered by municipalities, the first under the Electric Lighting Act of 1882, the second only to a slight extent under the Tramways Act 1870—since that Act gave power to the municipality only to provide the tramway but not run the carriages itself—and mostly therefore by Local Private Act.

Water-supply is now mostly in the hands of Local Authorities or in some areas Joint Boards representative of them. The supply of gas and of electricity was nationalized under national and regional 'public corporations' in 1948. During the present century trams have given way to omnibuses. The town Authorities which ran the former have obtained powers to run the latter, often around as well as in their areas, but inter-town and country services are largely in the hands of companies.

GROUP CHARACTERISTICS

It may be said with truth that in one way or another the development of municipal services reflects the whole play of social, economic, and political forces since the Industrial

Revolution; and it is not therefore to be supposed that the policies which govern these widely varied services exhibit the uniformity, and freedom from anomaly, of some *a priori* scheme, or that, as a consequence, the services can be neatly classified. There are indeed many inconsistencies in the legislative approach made in one service as distinct from that made in another, and in the rules which Parliament has prescribed for the conduct of the services by the Local Authorities. Generally speaking, however, we can distinguish four groups, with fairly well-marked characteristics.

The first we may call the Protective Services, of which the more obvious and important are the Police and Fire Services but which also include the wide miscellany of regulative and inspectoral work involved in sanitation, building regulation, the control of food supply, the checking of weights and measures, and such like functions. The conditions of the Police and Fire Services are nationally determined and prescribed, but these conditions are applied, and the Forces administratively controlled, by the Local Authorities, subject to some overriding control by the Home Secretary The State makes a specific grant to Local Authorities of half the expenditure incurred in the maintainance of local Police Forces, but the Fire Service grant was withdrawn in 1958. However, the Fire Service is indirectly subsidised by the new General Grant in aid of local rate funds that replaced many specific grants. In the case of the remaining duties in this sphere, the Local Authorities enjoy wider freedom from central supervision.

In the second group fall services such as sewering, sewage disposal, public cleansing, public lighting, and the provision and maintenance of streets and roads (except the Trunk Roads, for which the Ministry of Transport is responsible but which certain Local Authorities maintain as agents of the Ministry). I call these the Communal Services because all need them, all are served by them, and, on the whole, all use them as needed and pay for them collectively through the rates. Except for certain road grants, and grants for rural sanitation, etc. they are almost entirely sustained at the charge of the local rates. This situation is partly to be explained on historical grounds. Though services such as these were in reality the necessary condition or accompaniment of town life, they were usually started by voluntary associations of leading inhabitants in the new towns created by the Industrial Revolution, uniting to provide themselves with amenities which neither the State nor any existing organ of local government such as the reformed Municipal Corporations created by the Municipal Corporations Act of 1835 recognized any duty of its own to provide. These associations of leading inhabitants procured their own incorporation as Town Commissioners, with power to levy a rate for the particular service they were incorporated to provide, e.g. watching, paving, lighting, sewering. A rate was resorted to because a charge related to the exact measure of use was manifestly impossible; and because the real-property assessment on which the rate was based appeared to be a fairly satisfactory rough measure of the use and value the ratepayers would receive. The services were not at first carried into neighbourhoods which could not afford to pay the rate, and in those days most inhabitants of the new towns of the Industrial Revolution were too poor to afford such luxuries. Eventually, however, it became the policy embodied in the developing code of sanitary legislation to carry such services throughout the towns. Moreover, as local government developed, the several rates levied for services such as these were eventually consolidated into one General Rate along with the rate levied for Poor Law (originally levied because property assessment afforded a measure of ability to pay). These two circumstances now obscure the extent to which a general local rate may still in fact be levied according to use made of particular services or the benefit received from them. We may broadly say today that services such as these are communal in the fullest sense: the community serves every individual according to his need, and the individual makes return to the community according to his ability to pay. Having once been introduced at local charge, these services have remained so because it is the character of the locality which determines the extent to which they should be provided. Today the standard of services provided in the country-side steadily approaches that for long enjoyed in urban areas. Even so many villages of considerable size still do not have modern sewerage and are not prepared to pay for street lighting.

The third group of services may be called Social Services and comprises education and its associated medical services, housing, maternity and child welfare, and the welfare services such as the care of the aged, infirm, deaf, dumb, and blind, and of children lacking proper parental care. In services like these, large sections of the public are served considerably below cost; others not at all, or but slightly. The total cost is borne partly by the State out of national tax-revenue and partly out of local rates. The national taxes are largely levied according to ability to pay, without regard to the individual service which the State may render; and in respect of the services under consideration this is broadly true of the local rates. The poorer sections of the community are thus helped by the richer and provided with services they could not otherwise afford. Non-socialists justify this situation on the ground that we should retain the capitalist structure of industry as the best on all major counts but recognize its faults and correct them; and that the Social Services are the best corrective. Socialists would justify the situation by regarding the Social Services as, in essence, an award of compensation to those who suffer from an industrial system which distributes its awards unfairly without regard to real deserts, and creates mass poverty.

The fourth group is that of the Trading Services, comprising the provision of water, street transport, and in some places bridges, tunnels, or steam ferries. These, when in the hands of Local Authorities, are called Trading Services because of the commercial nature of the charges made for them and other financial features which mark the conduct of the service, which are in strong contrast with other groups. These services usually involve operations of an industrial character. They are maintained on a self-supporting basis without charge to the rates. They are capitalized, not out of the rates but by borrowings on a security thereof, constituting collateral security of a kind which usually ensures a supply of capital at very economic rates. The service is charged for on the commercial principle which relates the charge to individual use or service. To complete the analogy with the private trading enterprises, the trading undertakings often make a revenue surplus, or a net profit, which, if not applied in reduction of prices, is credited to a common good fund, available for the provision of general municipal amenities, or applied in relief of local rates—to the extent which Statute may permit.

CHAPTER II

The Structure

————————————

WE HAVE so far used the term 'Local Authority' in its most
general meaning. There are, however, as we have incidentally
mentioned, several kinds of Local Authority, some differing
from others only in a few features of their internal constitutions, other differing widely in respect of the areas they serve
and the services they conduct. The constitutions of the several
kinds of Authority will be dealt with in detail in Chapter V.
In the present chapter we describe the plan under which the
tasks of local government are allotted to the several types of
Authority and area. In other words, we survey here what has
come to be called, for lack of a better word, 'the structure' of
local government.

A GENERAL OUTLINE

The units in this structure are six in number—the County
Borough, the Administrative County, the Borough (often called
the Municipal or Non-County Borough to distinguish it from
the County Borough) the Urban District, the Rural District,
and the Parish. In addition, in the metropolitan area there are
the Greater London Council and the London Boroughs: as
shown below, distribution of functions between these
authorities differs from the normal county and non-county
borough pattern. There also exist some bodies specially
appointed for specific local purposes—*ad hoc* bodies as they are
called—and among these must be numbered the Joint Boards
and Joint Committees often formed by neighbouring Local
Authorities of the standard types for the purpose of co-operation in a particular service over adjoining areas. Our concern
here, however, is with the six units first-named, i.e. the
standard types.

The present structure was erected in stages during the last
century. The Municipal Corporation Act of 1835 reconstituted

the Boroughs on an elective basis; the Local Government Act of 1888 established a new kind of Borough called the County Borough, and also established the County Councils; and the Local Government Act of 1894 established the Urban, Rural, and Parish Councils, and fitted them, along with the Municipal (Non-County) Boroughs, into the framework of the Administrative County. The London County Council was set up at the same time as the other County Councils in 1888 (superseding the *ad hoc* Metropolitan Board of Works), but the metropolitan boroughs were not established until 1900, and even then the City of London was excepted in large measure, from the metropolitan structure, and the City Corporation's medieval constitution left virtually intact.

The most marked feature of the present structure is the difference between the unit and area known as the County Borough and all others. The County Borough—which is the unit formed by our big cities, most towns with a population above 75,000, and a few towns of less size—falls within the County geographically, but not for administrative purposes. As its name implies, the County Borough has, broadly speaking, the powers of a County and of a Borough, and this means that it carries on the full range of local government services within its boundaries. All other areas fall within the administrative County, which is subdivided into Boroughs, Urban Districts, and Rural Districts, the Rural Districts being further subdivided into Rural Parishes. In these County areas, as they are called, the services are divided among the County Councils, the Borough Councils, the Urban District Councils, the Rural District Councils, and the Parishes, certain services being allotted to each type of Authority. The Boroughs and Districts collect a Rate which covers the rate revenue required by the County as well as themselves.

Thus, while the citizen in a County Borough finds all services rendered by his County Borough Council, the citizen in a Borough, or in an Urban District finds some of his services provided by the Borough of Urban District Council, and others by the County Council. If he lives in some part of a Rural District he finds some services provided by the County Council, some by the Rural Council, and others by the Parish Council (or Meeting).

The Borough, Urban District, Rural District, and Parish

Councils are not subordinate to the County Council. Generally speaking, each type of Council within the County area is independently responsible for the range of functions allotted to it. In some services, however, the County Councils may, or must, delegate certain responsibilities to the Borough or District Councils, or use them as local executive agents.

The Municipal (Non-County) Boroughs and the Urban Districts (which differ in the constitution of their Councils but which both administer urban areas and have substantially the same range of function) run the greater number of services, mostly of the kind which we have described as communal, e.g. sewerage and sewage disposal, refuse collection and disposal, lighting and cleansing of streets, regulative public health, building regulation, parks, gardens, baths, allotments, etc. They are also housing authorities. Although that part of the cost of *classified* roads which is locally borne is spread over the County, and the cost of trunk roads is paid by the Ministry of Transport, the larger Boroughs and Urbans carry out the work of maintenance, repair, and improvement, and all Boroughs and Urban Districts control their own 'district' roads. Like the County Boroughs, many of the Boroughs and Urbans also undertake public utility services, such as water supply and street transport. Some of them which were above a certain population level at the crucial date also provided, until 1945, the elementary education and the maternity and child welfare services, and some Boroughs had their own police forces; but these functions are now (outside the County Boroughs) in the hands of the County.

Rural Councils' powers are of a similar character to those of the Urban Districts, but it is not necessary for them to provide amenities of the same character as are required in the towns. To deal with expanding villages they may acquire and apply urban powers.

The County Councils administer highways, fire brigades, ambulance services, primary, secondary, technical, and agricultural education, and the midwifery-maternity and domicidiary welfare services associated with the National Health Service, and have the care of the aged, infirm, deaf, dumb, and blind, and of orphans and children lacking parental care, under the National Assistance and Children Acts. They have a miscellany of licensing functions; and they join with Quarter Sessions in appointing a Standing Joint Committee which is the Police Authority outside the County Boroughs.

As from 1965 the pattern of local government in the London region is determined by the London Government Act, 1963. The new Greater London Council (G.L.C.) covers the territory of the London County Council, Middlesex, the county boroughs of Croydon, East Ham and West Ham together with parts of the adjacent Home Counties which form part of the London conurbation. Within this area local government functions are divided between the G.L.C., 32 London Boroughs and the Common Council of the City of London. The G.L.C. takes over services which demand large-scale organisation and unified control, e.g. fire prevention, licensing of theatres, ambulances and main drainage, while the Boroughs and the Common Council are responsible for personal and social services. Some tasks, notably housing, highways and planning, are shared between the two tiers of authority. The position about education is complex: in the inner area (the former L.C.C. area) the responsible body is a committee of the G.L.C., but outside the central zone the Boroughs become the local education authorities. London differs also from the rest of the country in that some services that commonly fall within the sphere of local government are organised in other ways either by 'ad hoc' bodies, the Metropolitan Water Board and the London Transport Executive, or by the national government which ultimately controls the Metropolitan Police through the Home Secretary.

In order that the reader may form a clear preliminary idea of the structure, we have not encumbered the foregoing outline with any full or detailed description of the distribution of powers and the exact range of each Authority's services; but as detailed a description as is necessary for the purposes of this work is embodied in Appendix A, which the reader is invited to study more closely after reading this chapter.

It will be useful at this stage to visualize the structure in bare outline. It rests upon a division of the country into areas of six kinds—the County Borough, the Administrative County, the Municipal (or 'non-county') Borough, the Urban District, the Rural District, and the Parish. The primary division is into County Boroughs and Administrative Counties, the Administrative Counties being sub-divided into Municipal Boroughs, Urban

Districts, and Rural Districts, and the Rural Districts further sub-divided into Parishes. The County Boroughs are the densely-populated areas of the larger towns, and although geographically situated within Counties they are detached for Local Government, and their Councils are 'all-purposes' Authorities. In the Administrative Counties functions and services are distributed. The Council of the Administrative Counties handle those requiring organization on a large-scale throughout their areas. In the Municipal Boroughs (smaller or medium-sized towns) the Urban Districts (built-up areas, often with the characteristics of the smaller town), and the Rural Districts (areas mainly rural) the Councils handle more localized tasks. The Parishes look after village amenities in the Rural Districts. There is thus one-tier local government in the County Boroughs, two-tier in the Municipal Boroughs and Urban Districts, and three-tier in the Rural Districts.

DISTINCTIONS—REAL AND NOMINAL

Despite the simplified description of a very complex structure which we have endeavoured to give in the foregoing outline, it is unlikely that this will have removed all misconceptions and confusion from the mind of the lay-reader. The piecemeal growth of the structure has left behind it, not only many anomalies and some needless complexities in the structure itself, but a most unfortunate confusion in the nomenclature associated with it. Where, the citizen may ask, is the place of the city in this structure? The answer is that the city has no place in it at all. The largest of our cities, such as Birmingham, Liverpool, Manchester, and Leeds, are no more, constitutionally, than County Boroughs. There is no higher rank for a large urban community than that of County Borough, if we disregard the Metropolis—which is so large that it was thought necessary to provide it with a two-tier structure rather than the unitary constitution of a County Borough. The term 'city' is merely a title of courtesy, a title which some people hold to have been accorded to a town which was originally the site of a cathedral or the seat of a bishop, but a title which, whether this explanation be true or false, can be conferred on any town today by Letters Patent of the monarch.

The distinction between a County Borough and a Municipal

(Non-County) Borough is a vital one, to some extent suggested by the words, and to some extent not. The vital distinction between the two is in respect of their range of powers and services. The County Borough is a self-contained unit, administering the full range of local government powers, i.e. practically speaking the combined powers of a County Council and of a Borough Council. On the other hand, the Municipal Borough (properly styled Borough without any prefix) is a division of the administrative County in which the County Council carries out some services itself, and the Borough Council others. Nevertheless, the Local Authority for both kinds of Borough—County and Non-County—has the same constitution, and this is the most highly developed one in local government, and one that gives the local community a prestige that the word Borough has conveyed since medieval times. Both types of Borough must originally have been created by grant of a Charter of Incorporation by the Crown. Some of our Boroughs possess Charters going back to the twelfth and thirteenth centuries, and these are still the warrant to their local government status as Boroughs, though their Councils are now constituted on the democratic pattern imposed by the Municipal Corporations Act of 1835 on all the Boroughs then existent, and by subsequent legislation (now consolidated in the Local Government Act of 1933) on all those since created.

There is no statutory level of population for the grant of a Charter, though in practice few Authorities of less than 20,000 will succeed in a Petition. Charters are formally granted by the Crown on the advice of the Privy Council, but in effect on the advice of the Ministry charged with local government affairs, which treats an application for a Charter as an occasion on which to review the general efficiency of the services and administration of the applicant Authority (a District, and usually an Urban District, Council) and advises a refusal if these are below standard. The step from Urban District to Borough status is a much easier and obviously less important one that that from ordinary Borough to County Borough status; since the latter means, we must once more emphasize, that the jurisdiction of the County is ousted, as the lawyers would say, and the town becomes a completely self-providing community for local government purposes.

The Act of 1888 which established the County Borough as a

unit of local government gave the status to towns of 50,000 population or more, and provided that towns attaining that size in future could be granted the status if their application were approved through Provisional Order procedure (See Chapter III). The Local Government (County Boroughs and Adjustments) Act 1926 raised the qualifying population level to 75,000 and provided that the status could only be granted by Local Private Act. The Local Government Act 1958 further raised the qualifying level to 100,000 and placed a ban on the promotion of Local Private Acts for 15 years. Under this Act, however, a comprehensive review of the status and areas of all Local Authorities has been set in train through the agency of a Local Government Commission (a development we shall be discussing later). In this review a presumption is to arise that a population of 100,000 is sufficient to sustain County Borough status—though population will not be the only consideration.

We are now brought to the question of the difference between a Borough and an Urban District, and the short answer is that the internal constitution of the Local Authority, i.e. the Borough Council, differs from that of the Urban District in ways which we shall more fully describe in Chapter V, and that the status of a Borough is one of higher prestige. The powers of the two types of Local Authority are practically the same. The Boroughs have an historic right, continued by legislation, themselves to make By-laws for Good Rule and Government, as well as for the suppression of nuisances, subject, of course, to the necessary confirmation of the Minister concerned; and although the County Council has a similar power, it must exclude any of the Boroughs within its administrative area from the scope of any County By-laws of this kind. On the other hand, an Urban District Council has no power to make By-laws of this wider type, although it had power to make By-laws for certain specified purposes, particularly under the Public Health Acts.

The differences between an Urban District and a Rural District do not call for much comment as the terms clearly indicate that the types of area served are different, or supposed to be different. The Rural District has not quite the same general powers to provide services of the communal types as is possessed by the Urban District. To provide, however, for the growth of Parishes and for urbanized 'pockets', the Rural Districts can

c

be empowered by the appropriate minister to apply in specified portions of their area certain powers which accrue automatically to Urban Districts.

A final distinction which should be noted is that between the Rural Parish and the Urban Parish. It is now only the Rural Parish which is an administrative unit of local government, in the sense that it is served or governed by its own Parish Meeting or Parish Council. The Urban Parish remains, however, a working area for the purposes of registration of births, deaths, and marriages; but its boundaries are now generally made to conform, as change and development occur, to the boundaries of the Boroughs and Urban Districts.

In the light of the foregoing classification it will be agreed that the nomenclature in use is not one which lets meaning shine through it; and it is the more regrettable, therefore, that the consolidating Local Government Act of 1933 should have made confusion worse confounded by introducing the further term 'County District'. This is the generic name given in that Act to Boroughs, Urban Districts, and Rural Districts alike, to indicate them as units of the administrative County.

THE AREA PATTERN

The Administrative County is a County from which the islands representing the County Boroughs have been taken out; otherwise its boundaries follow those of the geographical County. Exceptionally, Yorkshire is divided into three Administrative Counties, namely, the East, West, and North Ridings. Lincoln also is divided into three Administrative Counties: Holland, Kesteven, and Lindsey. Suffolk and Sussex are divided into West and East parts, as separate Administrative Counties. The mainland of Hampshire forms one Administrative County and the Isle of Wight another. Except for these special divisions, the County boundaries adopted when the Local Government Act of 1888 set up the County Councils were virtually those which had existed since the Norman Conquest; and apart from the out-growth of some County Boroughs these boundaries have largely remained static, though the areas of most other units have changed considerably. London, of course, is a special case. It is not one of the historic Counties, but has absorbed Middlesex and parts of the neighbouring

Home Counties physically and now also for the purpose of local administration.

Administrative Counties show remarkable divergencies in size. Lancashire has a population of over 2 million; Rutland has only 26,000. The typical County is diverse in character, being predominantly rural, but including substantial urbanized areas, represented by the Non-County Boroughs and Urban Districts—some of which have grown to great size without assuming higher status or dropping out of their administrative counties, as would happen if they became County Boroughs.

Diversity in population is equally a characteristic of County Boroughs which number about 80.[1]

Although, as already mentioned, the future norm for the creation of a County Borough is to be 100,000 inhabitants, over a third of the towns in this category have less. Canterbury has a mere 30,000. On the other hand, almost a score of them have populations about 200,000. They are all compact urban communities.

There are about 300 Non-County Boroughs of which roughly three dozen have populations between 5,000 and 10,000, and nearly 50 have populations below 5,000; and of these latter almost a score are even less than 2,500. Montgomery is the smallest with 880 inhabitants. These small Boroughs are mostly ancient centres, of considerable rank and importance in the age before the Industrial Revolution, but which were eclipsed by the manufacturing towns which then developed. At the other extreme, a few have populations above or bordering on 100,000 and these are commonly the towns which clamour for County Borough status. The 32 new Metropolitan Boroughs are more equal in size with an average population around a quarter of a million. The City of London with 5,000 residents is, of course, the supreme anachronism in British local government.

There are about 550 Urban Districts. Nearly half have less than 10,000 inhabitants while a handful approach the 100,000 mark.

The number of small units is specially noticeable in this class, 122 being below 5,000 inhabitants,—less than town-planners today think a minimum size for a neighbourhood

---

1. It is useless to give a precise figure for the number is constantly changing as the process of structural reform continues.

unit. A handful of these authorities are even below the 1,000 mark and Llanwrtyd Wells U.D.C. is the smallest with a tally of 490.

There are about 470 Rural Districts; 5 of them cover areas of over 200,000 acres—greater than the individual areas of 6 County Councils. Populations in no case exceed 100,000, and about four-fifths of this group fall between the 5,000 and 30,000 limits, but 36 are below 5,000 .

There are 7,400 Parishes with Councils; and nearly 4,000 Parishes governed by Meetings only.

Exclusive of these, the Local Authorities in England and Wales number 1,530 (not counting *ad hoc* bodies) and nearly two-thirds of them have populations of less than 20,000 and some 250 have populations less than 5,000.

The table in Appendix B, showing the populations of these Local Authorities (excluding the Parishes), may contribute to a general idea of the pattern of local government in the country.

WHAT TESTS SHOULD STRUCTURE SATISFY?

In Chapter IX there is a survey of the defects in this structure and a review of the more important of recent proposals for change, and the policy and action recently decided upon by Parliament to rehabilitate it. Our task here is to explain it; and we cannot do this merely by describing its exterior features. We must form some idea of the ends which a local government structure should serve, and the conditions it must meet; and we must then disengage the plan on which this particular structure was designed to meet those ends and conditions. Even then we shall not understand the structure very well—and still less be able to decide whether we need to improve it or to replace it—if we do not learn to distinguish between the plan and the application (or misapplication) of the plan. First, then, as to the ends which a structure of local government should serve, and the conditions to be met.

Within the scope of an individual Local Authority's responsibilities there is room for a differentiation between functions of 'policy' and 'administration'; but from a broad national standpoint the work of Local Authorities is administrative and executive. They apply and administer policies which are prescribed or authorized, and in some measure defined, by Parliament. The major aim in a local government structure must be therefore, in broad terms, an administrative aim. The structure is fittingly conceived of in administrative terms; and it is to administrative tests that it must finally be brought. The citizen is to be served; and the primary aim of the machinery of local democracy should be to serve him with maximum efficiency and economy. 'With economy' does not mean that the citizen is to be served as cheaply as possible, but as cheaply as is consistent with efficiency and a given standard of provision. 'With efficiency' implies, in the sphere of local public service, responsiveness to the citizen's needs, and the minimum of vexation, consistently, again, with the standards or methods laid down. The ability to assimilate new tasks must also be definitely marked out as one of the most important aspects of local government efficiency.

How can structure affect and condition aims such as these? In great part, it is true, they depend on the Local Authority's own calibre and organization. Yet the influence of structure may be profound. Many if not all of the requirements which the citizen makes upon the agencies of local government form an economic complex: the citizen wants one service with another, and each related to the other, and it is desirable and perhaps imperative, particularly if the services are of cognate kinds, that one agency should supply all—a course which, as we notice later, is usually the more economical. In these considerations is grounded the preference given in modern times to the principle of establishing Local Authorities which administer a number of services—a principle which, on the whole, informs the present structure.

Again, the area over which a Local Authority operates determines the 'size' of the local service, conceived of as an administrative unit, and this in turn may profoundly affect the levels of economy and efficiency on which the service can be carried on. Local government services are no differently affected by the Law of Increasing Return than business undertakings. There must be lower limits of size which, even if they allow of a fairly effective technical lay-out, result in high overheads or unnecessary duplication of plant, institutions or staff by comparison with those which would suffice over a feasible larger area, embracing existing smaller areas. There must be upper limits of size at which economies secured in these ways begin to be offset by difficulties of control and supervision, by costly and intricate checks, balances, and devices for control, and by rigid standardization of practice, all of which are the vices of the super-scale unit everywhere. There is no doubt an optimum size for each service which is different in every case; and most experienced local government administrators recognize broad groupings of services which require larger or smaller areas. In these conditions, unless we countenance a system in which there will be a Local Authority for each service, it becomes important to make as appropriate a grouping of services as possible. Apart altogether from the influence of size in administrative economy, it is possible for areas to be too small to possess the financial resources necessary to maintain a service adequately—i.e. with a proper standard of provision for the local inhabitants, and with an adequate and well-qualified staff such as is indispensable to efficiency.

It is manifest from what has been said already, that the way in which a given locality must be catered for by a local government structure is dependent on a balance of considerations. There are, however, still further aims and conditions to meet than those mentioned so far—which spring from the nature of the services. Irrespective of the best areas for administration we may have to pay regard to the areas over which the charge should be spread; which ought to be small if the benefit of the services accrues mainly to a localized community (e.g. urban amenities such as street lighting), or larger if the benefits are diffused (e.g. classified roads), or if the charge requires pooling (e.g. educational and welfare services in County areas).

And finally, we must remember that we have to find suitable areas for the control of local government services by the representatives of the public. This means that the electoral areas must be feasible ones for the purpose of local elections and allow easy contact between the public representative and his constituents, and between him and the Local Authority's Officers and Departments. These latter considerations are factors by no means extraneous to considerations of administrative efficiency. The executive agents of the Local Authority, i.e. its Officers, must do their work under the effective control and supervision of the public representatives, who constitute the Local Authority for the area; and in many respects the degree in which this control and supervision can be effective is dependent on the suitability of the areas chosen for the election and constitution of the Local Authority, quite apart from any area requirements of the services themselves.

These further considerations do but emphasise the fact—not always appreciated by those who look merely for the ideal arrangement in the administration of one particular service—that the particular way in which a given locality should be fitted into a general structure of local government results from an equation of the administrative needs and area-characteristics of the services—which may vary considerably—the requirements of financial charge, and the conditions necessary to secure public control.

THE CONCEPTIONS UNDERLYING
THE PRESENT STRUCTURE

As we have already indicated, the present structure grew piecemeal. It is therefore not to be supposed that it embodies a completely logical and pre-established conception of what a local government structure should be. A conception of what was needed was only gradually formulated as new social requirements arose in the last century and in the light of the experience obtained in meeting them. There developed, however, in the latter part of the last century certain lines of thought which shaped the structure to its present form.

First, the view gradually established itself that it is better to have a system of 'compendious' Local Authorities, each exercising an appropriate variety of functions rather than one in which each service is conducted by a separate authority established for that purpose alone, i.e. a system of 'ad hoc' authorities.

Secondly, it was believed necessary to follow the pattern of town and country; and for the most part to differentiate between the two kinds of areas by providing separate Authorities for each. Apart from any supporting philosophy the administrative observance of town-and-country pattern was obviously the line of least resistance in the upgrowth of services and agencies forced by the Industrial Revolution. Though segregation of town and country has been criticized as now

both unnecessary and undesirable there is no general accep-
tance of such a view as yet.

Thirdly, it was deemed necessary to let local communities
which were recognizably separate and distinct, even though
not remote from each other, bear the cost of their own services,
in view of the different levels of provision necessary in different
areas or the distinctive character of the amenities suited to such
areas. This outlook obviously fortified, if it was not indeed part
of, the philosophy which felt it necessary to distinguish between urban and rural areas.

Fourthly, a recognition grew up latterly that, outside the
largest towns, the compendious machinery should be such as
would accommodate some services which required a large, and
others which required a smaller area, either for purposes of
control, administration or the purpose of defraying the cost of
the service.

Let us review these considerations in turn.

The gradually perceived compendious principle of organization did not fructify until late in the nineteenth century. From
the beginning of the Industrial Revolution until then, the new
local government services were provided by a host of *ad hoc*
Authorities, not because that principle of organization was
consciously preferred, but because, in the circumstances of the
time, it was usually the only one possible. Thus, although the
Municipal Corporations Act of 1835 created the first elements
in the modern structure, namely, the Boroughs, by providing
them with a democratic constitution, many of the services in
the reformed Boroughs still continued to be run by the bodies
of Paving, Lighting, and Watching Commissioners such as we
mentioned in Chapter I. The Act of 1835, moreover, provided
no machinery for the constitution of new Boroughs, and large
new communities which sprang up still continued to be catered
for by Commissioners. Again, one of the early reforms of highways administration in 1835 created special Highway Boards,
and the Public Health legislation which began with the Public
Health Act of 1848 established separate Boards of Health;
though in many cases these did absorb some of the bodies of
Improvement, etc., Commissioners. In fact, it is safe to say that
it was the variously named bodies of Town Commissioners, and
the Highways and Health Boards, which were in most places
the true precursors of the modern municipality, rather than the

ancient Corporations abolished in 1835.

The Poor Law likewise continued to be administered under the *ad hoc* bodies named the Guardians of the Poor set up in 1834, the areas of administration having been built up into combinations of Parishes called 'Unions'—(hence the name 'The Union' given to the Poor Law Institution until the reforms of the present century). And even when a public system of education was established by the Education Act of 1870, the local administration had to be given to *ad hoc* School Boards. The situation as it existed in the 'seventies was described in a famous debate preluding the legislation of 1888 and 1894, as 'a chaos of authorities, a chaos of areas, and, still worse, a chaos of rates'.

The situation was, as we have seen, dealt with by the legislation of 1888 and 1894, which gave to the largest towns the unitary constitution of the County Borough as an embodiment of the compendious principle in its highest development, and which grouped the services in the County areas around the Counties, Boroughs, or Districts, and to a minor degree the Parishes. Even so, it took some time to clear up the remnants of the older system. Thus the School Boards were not abolished until the Education Act of 1902, which divided elementary education between the Administrative County, and the Boroughs with a population of 10,000 at the last Census, and the Urban Districts with a population of 20,000—the County Council becoming the Authority for secondary education everywhere throughout the County. And it was not until the reforms of 1929 that the Guardians of the Poor were abolished, and the functions transferred to the Counties and the County Boroughs, with provision that, in the County areas, the County should work through a series of local Committees called Guardians Committees.

In general, we may say that the compendious principle has obvious advantages in economy of administration through the possibility it offers of co-ordinating one service with another, and the flexibility and resourcefulness for new tasks necessarily possessed by a unit assembling a multi-competent staff for widely varying functions. The principle is carried to its greatest extent in the County Boroughs.

The virtues of the County Borough type of government are impressive. Each service has a 'market' of dimensions and character such as allow easy contact between 'producer' and 'consumer', quick executive action on the spot, close knowledge of consumers' requirements, and effective supervision by Council and Management—the Council itself being an effective focal point for reference to, and by, the Management in dealing with consumers' needs and complaints. As we have said, the wants of the citizens are often a complex which can be met only by the closest co-operation of one service with another; and the organism of the County Borough offers the possibility of such a co-operation as does no other. Since the Departments which cover the whole range of services provided to the public are grouped together, it is easy for one to contact and help another; and these factors and the variety of the total staff engaged make the organism prehensile, and singularly well adapted to new tasks. At the same time the juxtaposition of Departments makes for economy all round; central establishments, such as legal and financial, serving the executive departments such as the engineering and the architectural, and these, in turn, advising and serving the administration. Finally, the whole organism is under a unified control which brings the public representative and the expert into the closest and most frequent contact (owing to the compactness of the area). This, and the visibility of local action to the local public, effectively preclude the growth of bureaucratic outlook and habit. In brief, the organism has the highest degree of elasticity, resource, economy, and responsiveness to public need; and these spring essentially from that concentration of many-sided activity under unified local control which is the characteristic of this— the most highly developed—type of English Local Government administration. It is manifest that it is easier to achieve this type of organization in a substantial area of uniform urban development such as the County Boroughs, than in the mixed area of the County Council; but even where the services are divided, as in the County areas, the grouping of services between the larger or smaller units of County or County District, however imperfect, is still a better arrangement than the disintegration of local government administration by the *ad hoc* principle. Under the present plan, co-ordination between one Authority and another, in the County areas, is not easy. Under the other system it would be impossible everywhere.

As to the segregation of urban and rural communities, the

possibility as well as the desirability of administering units of
mixed character such as the Administrative County as though
they were County Boroughs has been advocated in recent
years. Such an arrangement was not thought possible at the
time of the legislation of 1888 and 1894. It is to be remembered,
however, that in that epoch urban communities not suitable for
County Borough status were nevertheless on a higher level of
local government development than the rural areas. Until 1888
the rural areas were still under the government of the Justices
of the Peace, working through the ecclesiastical vestries. It was
a matter of expediency to preserve the identity of these urban
elements, even though small, for most of them, though they
were then coming under a compendious form of Borough or
Urban government, had existed, as communities, for many
years, under the rule of Commissioners, Boards of Highways,
or Boards of Health, and possibly of all three.

The considerations outlined in the foregoing paragraph were
much fortified by the feeling that the urban communities
should pay for their own amenities, and that where these
amenities were not needed, or were needed on a less scale, as
in the rural areas, there should be a separate area of charge
and consequently of responsible administration.

As to the aim of accommodating both large-scale and small-
scale services, it should be noted that the County Councils took
over from the Justices (until 1888 the Local Authorities of the
rural areas—exercising administrative as well as judicial functions) services such as roads and bridges, which were hardly
capable of administration on the basis of the smaller unit. The
initial range of the functions of County Councils was very
narrow indeed; but they appear to have been established with
some foresight that both existing or new services might require
a larger unit. This expectation was first justified by the education service at the beginning of the century. The institutions
required for secondary education were obviously of a kind
which must serve areas wider than many of the Boroughs and
Districts; and in the purely rural and small urban areas the
siting of even elementary schools sometimes required the areas
of the smaller units to be transcended. In 1929, it was decided
to transfer Poor Law functions to the compendious Local
Authorities, because outside the County Boroughs the wider
unit of the County was essential for efficient and impartial

administration and also to secure an adequate spread of the charge. Larger units also assist more uniform standards of provision and, by enabling the employment of specialised staff, improve technical competence. Such considerations prevailed when the classified roads were transferred to County administration by the Act of 1929 with provision for the exercise of delegated powers of maintenance, repair, etc., by the larger of the Urban Authorities in the County areas; and in the post-war transfers of town and country planning, police, fire-brigades, and the various welfare services. The functions of the County Councils have grown considerably throughout the first half of this century, and in recent years at the expense of the Boroughs and Districts.

The larger Boroughs and Districts, however, have enjoyed some recompense as they are allowed to administer some county services through the technique of delegation. Education provides the leading example of this trend. Under the Education Act, 1902, the Counties shared the provision of schooling with the larger Boroughs and Urban Districts: Boroughs with a population of 10,000 in 1901 and Urban Districts of 20,000 were responsible for elementary education. The 1944 Education Act ended this division of function by centralisation at county level, but a town with 60,000 population—or exceptionally a little less—could apply for what is known as 'excepted district' status which grants the local council fairly wide powers to deal with the day-to-day educational administration within their area. Smaller towns may be grouped together with Rural Districts to perform similar but more limited duties in units known as 'divisional executives': this arrangement is most common in the larger Counties. In the same way the task of dealing with applications for permission to develop land may be delegated to any Borough or District. The Local Government Act, 1958, added health and welfare services to the list of functions that were to be delegated to Boroughs and Districts in the 60,000 class. The amount of delegation within Counties is now, therefore, quite considerable, and two aspects of it are of special importance. First, it is always the case that a County retains overall financial responsibility for delegated functions which remain a charge on the county rate. Thus the County can issue policy directives which control the use made of the delegated powers. Second, there is now a considerable difference between the duties of a Borough or Urban District above 60,000 population and the work of the local authorities in the smaller towns, for above the 60,000 mark the local Town Hall becomes responsible for the current provision of the major social and educational services.

CHAPTER III

The Constitutional Setting

To A GREATER extent than in in most other countries, local government in England has meant local *self*-government. In many modern States, even before the advent of totalitarian régimes, there was local government, but little local *self*-government. Local government was largely in the hands of local emissaries of the central government. Elected local Councils existed, but their powers were narrow, and they were subordinate, in France to Prefects, and in other countries to State officers of a similar kind, in a measure which we have not countenanced in this country, even under the war-time régime of Regional Commissioners.

A sovereign democratic State must always, however, set some limits to the autonomy of local bodies; and even in England we find all three organs of State power—Legislature, Judiciary, and Executive—exercising some control over the activities of the Local Authorities.

PARLIAMENTARY CONTROL

The most fundamental form of central control is that which is exercised by Parliament. Except in a sense so narrow as to be negligible, Local Authorities are not legislative bodies. They are executive bodies exercising powers, or discharging duties, given to them by Parliament, as the sovereign legislative assembly; and the rule is virtually absolute that they may exercise no powers at all except such as Parliament has given. This fact is not always appreciated by the public, or by those who seek to serve on Local Authorities. Perhaps because they are democratically elected by the citizens at large, in each locality, Local Authorities are sometimes referred to as 'local Parliaments'. The term is deceptive. A Local Authority is very far indeed from being a local Parliament. Though it can sometimes choose whether or not to do something it has power to do, though it is largely (but not entirely) free to choose the particular manner in which it will do something which it has power to do, the objects it pursues must be such as Parliament has authorized; and Parliament has frequently gone so far as to lay down, or to authorize a Minister of the Crown to lay down, the lines on which the Local Authority must pursue such objects. The Local Authority cannot do anything which it is not authorized to do by Act of Parliament. It is this rule which lawyers have in mind when they speak of Local Authorities as 'creatures of statute'.

Parliamentary authority accrues to the Local Authorities in a variety of ways. Some powers are given to them in the Acts which established them. Some are given to them generally, or to certain categories among them, by general legislation from time to time. In both these cases legislation takes the form of a Public General Act and usually originates in a Government measure. Optional powers are sometimes given by a Public General Act known as an Adoptive Act, which can be 'adopted' by a Local Authority by resolution. Parliament passes this kind of Act to cover cases where the powers should be optional, but, if used at all, should be exercised on the same lines wherever they are in fact exercised. An instance is the Small Dwellings Acquisition Act 1899, which has enabled so many thousands of citizens to acquire the ownership of their homes through municipal loans.

It is the practice of Governments, before framing general measures affecting the Local Authorities, to consult them through their organized associations, namely, the County Councils Association, the Association of Municipal Corporations, the Urban District Councils Association, the Rural District Councils Association and the National Association of Parish Councils.

Other powers are given to individual Local Authorities on their own application by what are called Local Private Acts. Parliament usually grants Local Private Acts for peculiar local purposes; but, in some instances, though reluctant to confer powers on Local Authorities at large, Parliament has been willing to grant them if local conditions are deemed satisfactory, and therefore makes the grant of powers by Local Private Act after reviewing local conditions. The Bills for these Acts are 'promoted' by the Local Authority desiring the powers, and though the Bill must pass the usual Parliamentary stages of three readings in each House, it is customary not to debate the Bills in the House, but to leave them to be considered by a specially selected small Committee of the House in which they are introduced. The proceedings before the Committee assume a quasi-judicial character, the promoters putting forward their case by way of evidence, and being usually represented by Counsel practising at the Parliamentary bar; petitioners against the grant of the powers being called upon to appear and put forward evidence in objection.

A somewhat similar though simpler procedure is often available when powers are desired of a kind which are fairly commonly in demand. Parliament is often willing in such cases to leave the process of investigation, and the initial decision, to the appropriate Minister, acting on the advice of expert advisers, though it reserves the right to approve or disapprove the Order he makes. The older form in which Parliament authorizes procedure of this kind is the Provisional Order. Each session the Provisional Orders made by the appropriate Minister, usually after a public Local Inquiry, are scheduled to a Provisional Orders Confirmation Bill, which is then put through the same Parliamentary stages as any other Bill, and which, if it passes, takes effect as an Act confirming the Order made by the Minister. The system obviates the comparatively elaborate and expensive procedure by Local Private Bill before a Parliamentary Committee, and rests on an understanding that Parliament will not upset the Minister's Provisional Order except on some question of major principle.

A new avenue of local powers became available through the increasing resort of Parliament, in recent years, to delegated legislation. In recognizing some sphere of public service or administration as one appropriate to local responsibility, Parliament has frequently empowered a minister to make enabling Orders of various kinds on the application of an individual Local Authority. Such 'statutory orders' are subject to procedures which require Parliamentary scrutiny, ratification, or approval, before they became effective, but all these procedures stop short of those necessary for an Act of Parliament.

While delegated legislation has been a source of enabling powers for Local Authorities, it has also been a new medium of prescription for the conduct of local government services, both old and new. The kind of prescription, legislative rather than administrative, which Parliament wrote into its own Local Government Acts in earlier days is in these days written into statutory orders, rules, and regulations, and on the whole written into these latter in infinitely greater detail. In measures designed for local administration, detailed legislative prescription tends in itself to be administrative prescription; but, be this as it may, there can be no doubt in point of fact that delegated legislation in the sphere of local government has been the medium not only for newer forms of legislative control but for new forms of administrative central control; and if we notice it here under the former heading it falls to be noticed again in this chapter under the latter.

JUDICIAL CONTROL

Parliamentary control is safeguarded by effective judicial sanctions. Any citizen can challenge an action which is *ultra vires* (outside the scope of the Local Authority's Parliamentary authorization) by application to the High Court for an injunction; and it is one of the functions of the Attorney-General to take up, on behalf of the citizen, any case of this kind which he considers to call for the exercise of the Court's jurisdiction. Most actions of a Local Authority affect the interests of some private citizen, or group of citizens, and the actions of Local Authorities are therefore systematically and closely watched by the interests affected. It is manifest that acts and policies of Local Authorities which go beyond the national will as expressed in Acts of Parliament can thus be effectively restrained. It should be appreciated, however, that when, in virtue of these powers, the Courts are said to 'act as watchdogs over the Local Authorities', this does not mean that they actively interest themselves continuously in the discharge of the Local Authorities' responsibilities. Consistently with the principle that they do not decide hypothetical cases, they are not self-motive even when they can scrutinize the legality of a Local Authority's actions. They act when moved to do so by an aggrieved litigant.

In general they cannot interfere with the particular way in which the Local Authority discharges its lawful powers, pro-

D

vided that way is itself *intra vires*, and lawful in any other respect—questions which will depend on what the authorizing legislation lays down, or is interpreted to lay down. In certain important matters, however, wherein a citizen's property or personal liberties may materially be affected by the administrative acts of a Local Authority, Parliament has provided the citizen with a right of appeal, sometimes to the appropriate Ministry, sometimes to the local Magistrates Court. It is not always practicable for appeals of this kind to be heard by the Ministry; but the Local Authorities often prefer such appeals to go to the Ministry, since they usually call for a technical or administrative knowledge which the local benches of lay magistrates do not possess.

Apart from special powers given to them for their specific tasks, Local Authorities are as much subject to the general civil law as the ordinary citizen. For example, they are liable for civil wrongs and breaches of contract in their relations with the individual citizen or those who do business with them.

ADMINISTRATIVE CONTROL

Neither Parliamentary nor judicial control has changed fundamentally in the upgrowth of modern local government. In character and scope they remain substantially what they were in the beginnings of the modern system. With some allowance, in the case of Parliamentary control, for the more detailed prescription which characterizes the legislation effected through statutory rules and orders, the same might even be said of the degree of control exercised by Parliament and the Courts.

The field of central administrative controls, i.e. those exercised by the central government through its ministers and their departments, presents a very different picture. Their general character has changed radically, in a piecemeal but extensive development of new forms and methods; their scope has widened, through their application, in one form or another, to more and more services; and although their incidence is still uneven and considerably less upon some services than upon others, the measure of their overall impact is infinitely greater than it was.

On this general situation we defer comment until later, and

pass to review the major forms and methods now in vogue.

The first is that which arises through the requirement for ministerial sanction to the borrowing of monies for capital purposes. New works, buildings or other assets which will benefit the ratepayers over a long period should not be charged to the rate for a short period such as a year: if the necessary money is borrowed and repaid over a period, the burden on the rate can be spread over time. Ministerial permission for such borrowing has always been required, but the reason for imposing this control has changed.

Originally, the requirement for loan-sanction was imposed so that Ministers could ensure that local schemes were both reasonable in terms of local financial resources and also technically sound. Since 1939 the Government has exercised general supervision over the national economy. In war-time this was essential to secure the distribution of resources needed for the proper organisation of the war effort. In peace-time it is necessary since the Government now assumes responsibility for the overall well-being of the economy, which demands a healthy balance of payments and high levels of employment and productivity. To this end, the total of capital expenditure allowed to all public authorities is fixed each year, and local authorities receive a ration from this amount. Thus local authorities have to fit into a national economic plan, and the amount of capital resources they are allowed to consume in any period will depend upon Government policy.

The system is undoubtedly a safeguard for smaller authorities which do not command a specialized staff, since the Minister maintains his own specialists to advise him on the merits of the local authorities' proposals. It also acts as a check to rash or ill-considered schemes. A Ministry dealing with the applications of many local authorities will obviously acquire much useful comparative knowledge of the lines on which authorities in general are meeting their problems; and the system is one, therefore, which brings such knowledge to bear upon each Authority's proposals. It may also promote an economical co-operation among local authorities, e.g. the Ministry may decline sanction for new works on the ground that the additional service could be secured by arrangement with an adjoining Authority. There are many who consider that the Ministry's control should be less meticulous or exercised on different lines, but there are few who would not agree that some degree of central Ministerial control is requisite.

The Ministry has power to aid its consideration of an application for loan-sanction by holding a public local Inquiry, of which notice is given by public advertisement and at which objectors may be heard. The local Inquiry fulfils, to some extent, the objects of a referendum, while avoiding the objections to that device which have made it rare in English constitutional practice. Besides enabling a fuller sifting of the facts by the Engineering Inspector who usually presides at these Inquiries, it enables the Ministry to detect any violent divergence between the Council and the feelings of the local public at large, and to be more fully apprised of the way in which any private rights may be affected by the Local Authority's proposals. It is usually only resorted to in cases of major importance. The Local Authorities often welcome it as affording a fuller opportunity of explaining their needs and proposals to the local public, through the publicity usually given to the proceedings; but they sometimes complain, perhaps with less warrant now than in the past, that the proceedings tend to be too legalistic and lend themselves too much to mere obstruction. The expense of such Inquiries is also a reason for avoiding them if this can be done without injustice, since the Local Authority must pay the Ministry's costs and its own and may be ordered to pay other parties', and the total cost may therefore be considerable when legal advocates are engaged.

Further controls over expenditure—which indirectly bear also upon the local authority's policy and administration—accrue through the conditions attached to State grants towards the cost of local government services or functions.

To such of these grants as are given in aid of specific services, and in particular to those paid as a percentage of the local authority's expenditure on the service, the conditions involve ministerial approval to the level of expenditure, and a detailed scrutiny of the measures and policy which the expenditure covers. The Authority may often be legally free to accept a grant or not; but the onus of the services which it is in these days expected to maintain is such as to leave it little option, and if it accepts the grant it accepts it on the conditions attached. These commonly include ministerial power to withhold the grant or to reduce it, if any prescriptions of the Minister as to the conduct of the service are not observed, or if he is dissatisfied with the management of the service or the standards maintained in providing it.

Until the introduction of a general grant towards expenditure in 1929, it could be said that, apart from expenditure on services aided by specific grants, the expenditure of the local authorities on revenue, as distinct from capital, account was free of central control; and except for a limitation on the expenditure of Parishes expressed in terms of rate-poundage there is still no direct control over the level of rates which the local authority levies. While the block grant (now paid in the substituted form introduced by the Local Government Act 1958) does not involve a detailed scrutiny and control over the general expenditure of the authority such as conditions the grants towards specific services, the legislation contains a provision, in the nature of a drastic reserved power, for the Minister to reduce the grant to an individual Authority if satisfied that the Authority has not achieved or maintained reasonable standards in the provision of the relevant services, regard being had to the standards maintained in other areas; though it should be noticed that the Minister's action under this power is subject to the prior approval of the House of Commons.

The potential scope of the controls operating through conditions attached to grants in one form or another can be stressed by noting that over half of the local authorities' total non-trading expenditure was defrayed by State grants in one form or another.

A further medium of central control over expenditure, likewise capable of affecting local authority policy and administration, is secured by Government audit. This is not of universal application. It is compulsorily applied to the whole expenditure of authorities other than county boroughs and boroughs, and to that portion of the expenditure of these latter authorities which is aided by specific service grants. It is not a mere accountancy audit; the Government's district auditor, as he is called, being charged with the duty of reviewing the legality of the expenditure which comes under his notice and directed to disallow all expenditure 'contrary to law'. He has powers of surcharging improper expenditure on those he deems responsible for it. We discuss this system later, but here we may note that it has three aspects. First, it represents a ministerial service performed for the local authority in lieu of other forms of audit. Secondly, it places the district auditor in a quasi-judicial position, particularly in respect of the test of legality—in the first instance at any rate, there being provisions for the review of his decisions by the Minister or the Courts. And thirdly, since the law itself has imported into the expression 'contrary to law' a rubric that expenditure can be 'contrary to law' if it is excessive or unreasonable (and not merely if it is illegal in its nature, or *ultra vires*) the system obviously places the auditor in a position in which local authority policy, as reflected in expenditure, comes within his purview.

In rather a different category from the three controls just described come others, too numerous and varied to classify, which reside in ministerial power to prescribe or direct as to the manner in which the local authority shall exercise some function or manage some service. Many of the prescriptions are effected through statutory rules, regulations or orders (which may require some form of Parliamentary ratification); for the content of these is seldom confined to prescription of a purely legislative character but extends to the executive aspect of the local authority's functions and services. In some cases indeed the local authority is directed to prepare administrative schemes for the exercise of its functions, for approval by the Minister. Ministerial Circulars of advice that have no statutory basis are now of increasing importance: indeed, any significant development in the work of local authorities is likely to be accompanied by a Circular. Also, as is shown below in the section entitled "Statutory Officers", Ministers may, in many cases, influence the appointment and dismissal of local government officials.

In recent Acts, dealing with services more national than local in character, e.g. the Education Act of 1944, Parliament has used statutory language which makes it clear that the local authority is little more than an executive agent for the conduct of the service. In this Act, for example, the Minister is directed to 'promote' the education of the people and 'to secure the effective execution by local authorities, under his control and direction', of the national policy. He is given an active rôle rather than a passive one, and endowed with powers of initiative and direction; whereas, under older conceptions of the central-local relationship in the conduct of such services, the Minister's rôle was conceived of more as one of final authority. The recent insistence by the Minister of Education that he should determine the level of teachers' salaries, if need be over-ruling the views of local authorities themselves, is one more example of the strength of ministerial supervision. Again, the Police Act, 1964, illustrates the tendency to augment national control.

Finally, we may notice that over some services the Ministries maintain periodical inspection, e.g. police, education; that they often have power to hold inquiries into some phase or other of the local authority's activity, over and above their power to hold local inquiries in applications for sanction to loans; and that in some spheres the Minister can exercise what are called 'default powers'—i.e. if he finds that the local authority has failed to carry out functions, or to comply with regulations. he may appoint some other local authority, or indeed some other kind of agency such as a Commissioner, to take the functions over, or he may, indeed, take these over himself. The exercise of such default powers is, it should be said, rare in the extreme.

In general there is one Ministry—at present the Ministry of Housing and Local Government but for many years the Ministry of Health and, before that again, the Local Government Board—concerning itself with Local Government affairs; but certain other Government Departments such as the Ministry of Education, the (new) Ministry of Health, the Ministry of Transport, and the Home Office, are concerned with particular services or functions.

THE ASSOCIATIONS OF LOCAL AUTHORITIES

It is convenient here to notice the associations of local authorities and the important functions they perform. Each type of local authority has its own national association which provides its members with a collective voice. These organisations are five in number: the County Councils Association, the Association of Municipal Corporations, which covers both county boroughs and non-county boroughs, the Urban District Councils Association, the Rural District Councils Association and the National Association of Parish Councils. There are also two similar bodies specifically concerned with education; the

Association of Education Committees represents the local education authorities, and the National Association of Divisional Executives in Education has been formed by the authorities exercising education powers delegated by counties.

These national organisations have a variety of functions. They provide advice for individual local authorities. They give an opportunity to exchange opinions and experience about current problems. They provide representation on the wide variety of advisory bodies that are in some way connected with local government. The first four of the associations listed above nominate representatives to the various national joint councils which determine the salaries, wages and conditions of employment for all those on the payroll of local authorities. But the main task of these organisations is to negotiate with each other and with government departments about proposals to change the law or any administrative practices concerning local government. Every association is in touch with one or more M.P.s who may be asked, on appropriate occasions, to put forward in the House of Commons the point of view of a particular category of local authority. It is easy to overlook these activities and to underrate their significance, because much of the work is done in private and does not receive great publicity. In fact, government departments pay great heed to the views of local authority associations which often cause a Ministry to modify its policy. On questions related to reform in the structure of local government Ministers have been notably reluctant to introduce any fresh legislation without first obtaining broad agreement from the associations.

CHAPTER IV

The Financial Basis

THE REVENUE NEEDED by the Local Authority is derived from
(a) rates; *(b)* income from corporate property and estate; *(c)*
trading revenues and other income from charges for services
not wholly borne by rates; and *(d)* grants and subsidies by the
State.

THE RATE

The rate is a local tax levied at so much in the £ upon the
annual value of property which is beneficially occupied. It was
first levied for the relief of the poor, under the Statute of
Elizabeth of 1601 which established the Poor Law and provided
for its administration through Overseers. Later, as we saw in
Chapter I, rates were often levied for other local government
purposes by incorporated bodies of Paving, Watching, Lighting,
Sewering, etc., Commissioners, and by the new organs of local
government which eventually superseded them. In 1925 all
these rates were finally consolidated into one general rate. A
Rural District Council may still, however, levy a special rate in
addition to its general rate in order to meet the varying needs
of different parts of its area; but this special rate is in effect an
addition, chargeable in a particular place, to the general rate.
Most Local Authorities and companies supplying water charge
the domestic consumer a water rate. Such a rate is usually
levied on the basis of valuations established for the local
authority's general rate, and when charged by a Local Authority supplying water, is usually collected along with the general
rate, but it is in reality a separate rate, levied on the consumers of water as such, and not upon occupiers of premises as
such. In what follows, we speak exclusively of the rates levied
for general purposes of local government and not for water
supply.

The class of property which is liable to be rated, comprising
rateable 'hereditaments' as they are called, is virtually, but not

completely, identical with that class of property which lawyers speak of as 'real property', if we exclude incorporeal hereditaments such as easements. Certain properties are, however, wholly exempt from rates. Thus, under a policy of State assisance to agriculture, all agricultural land, after being partly exempt for many years, was, in 1929, exempted altogether. Land occupied by the Crown is also totally exempt; because the Crown, which is never liable under any statute unless specially named, was not named in the Statute of Elizabeth, and this legal exemption has persisted in successive legislation. In practice, however, the Treasury makes an equivalent contribution. Property used for or in connection with religious worship, public parks, sewers, lighthouses, buoys, beacons, sheds for housing invalid chairs, and the residences of ambassadors and their servants, are also exempt; and so are certain classes of machinery not deemed to be part of a hereditament. Almshouses and other properties used for charitable purposes enjoy a 50% reduction in the amount of rates payable, and rating authorities have a discretionary power to remit their rates altogether. This discretionary power to reduce or remit rates extends to other non-profit making institutions, e.g. social clubs and educational, literary and scientific bodies.

Apart from these exemptions, liability to the rate only attaches during beneficial occupation. There is no statutory definition of beneficial occupation, but there is a voluminous literature of judicial decision explaining and illustrating the sense in which it is to be understood. It is carefully to be distinguished from profitable occupation. Empty properties bear no rates if there is no beneficial occupation, but it should be appreciated that there may often be beneficial occupation of properties popularly conceived of as empty.

As a rule, the rate is levied not only in respect of occupation, but upon the occupier; but in cases where special difficulty arises in ascertaining the occupier, or where the property is to all intents and purposes a single hereditament with many constituent occupations, the legislation provides that the owner may be levied instead of the occupier. Thus a block of flats may be treated as a single hereditament in the occupation of the person receiving the rents, and he may be made rateable; and where a person rents the whole of a building and sub-lets a part or parts of it, but retains control of the front door, he too can be treated as owner and made rateable; and where property is used as an advertising station the person permitting such use may be rated, and if he is not traceable, the owner; and so long as furniture and appliances are left in a theatre it is regarded as occupied, and the liability for rates falls on the owner or term-lessee.

Apart from these provisions, the legislation empowers the Local Authority to decide that rates shall be paid by the owner instead of the occupier of properties up to £18 Annual Value (or a somewhat higher figure in certain areas), this provision being obviously designed to assist the Local Authorities to recover their rates, without undue expense, on small cottage property. In addition, a Local Authority and an owner of rateable properties are enabled to enter into agreements under which the owner can pay in lieu of the occupiers and receive certain discounts (called 'compounding allowances'), varying according to the level of responsibility which he assumes in undertaking to pay direct to the Local Authority. Thus, if he undertakes to pay the rates whether the premises are occupied or not, he is to be allowed a discount not exceeding 15 per cent.; if he undertakes to pay so long as the premises are occupied, 7½ per cent.; but if he merely undertakes to collect the rates as they become due from the occupier, 5 per cent. An owner who is liable to pay under a Local Authority decision relating to properties less in value than £18 (or the corresponding figure) is to receive a discount of 10 to 15 per cent. if he pays promptly; but he cannot also receive the allowances available under agreement. Similarly, although a Rating Authority has a general power to allow a discount of 2½ per cent. for prompt payment of rates, such a discount cannot be given to an owner in addition to any compounding allowances he may be receiving, whether these be payable under a decision to rate owners of properties under £18 per annum, or under agreement.

The Rating Authority may require a tenant, under-tenant, or lodger to pay his landlord's arrears of rates and then recoup himself out of the rent due to the landlord. Power is also given to the Rating Authority to remit or reduce rates on grounds of poverty. This power is in addition to that of the local Magistrates, in whose Court rates are recoverable, to decline to issue a warrant of commitment for non-payment of rates if satisfied that the failure to pay is due to circumstances beyond the defaulter's control, and to their power, if so satisfied, to remit payment entirely. Further, under the Rating (Interim Relief) Act, 1964, where a ratepayer has suffered an increase in his rate demand of more than 25% between 1962 and 1964, and claims to have incurred hardship thereby, he may be excused part of the rate by the rating authority.

THE RATING AUTHORITIES

From the introduction of the rate as a means of local taxation by the Statute of Elizabeth in 1601, until the year 1925, rates were made and collected by the Overseers of the Poor. The needs of the new Local Authorities were satisfied through the levy made by the Overseers for the requirements of the Boards of Guardians which succeeded to the local administration of the Poor Law in 1834, but whose functions were transferred to the County Boroughs and Counties in 1929 before the Poor Law was finally broken up by still later legislation.

The Rating and Valuation Act of 1925 provided new means of raising and collecting the general rate. This it did by leaving the modern Local Authorities to raise the rating revenue they required for their own functions. The rates are now actually levied by the County Boroughs, and in County areas by the Boroughs, Urban Districts, and Rural Districts. The requirements of the County Councils are met through the levy made by the Non-County Boroughs and Districts in the administrative County, these, with the County Boroughs, being the 'Rating Authorities'. Before the time comes to levy the rate, the County Councils issue to the Boroughs and Districts in their area what is called a 'precept' indicating their requirements for the forthcoming financial year, and the amount required by the County Council is then added to that which the Borough or District requires itself, so that the Boroughs and Districts can levy a total poundage which will satisfy the County Council's requirements as well as their own. Similarly, the requirements of the Parishes in the Rural Districts are included by the Rural District Council in its levy of a general rate, though here, as we have mentioned, there is power for the Rural District Council to levy a special rate in particular parts of its area.

Every general rate has to be made for a period commencing immediately after the expiration of the current rate. It may be made for such period as the Rating Authority may fix, and the period usually adopted by Local Authorities is a year, though some prefer half-yearly periods even when they frame their *estimates* of Income and Expenditure upon a yearly footing. The year of account for all Local Authorities runs from 1st April to 31st March, and the yearly rate is therefore usually levied to commence 1st April and a half-yearly rate at 1st October. Supplementary rates may be made at any time if the Local Authority thinks it necessary. The principles to be observed in making the rate, and the practice and procedure which lead to the settlement of the rate, will be discussed in Chapter VII.

VALUATION

The rate is levied, as we saw, upon the Annual Rateable Value of properties. The valuation of all classes of hereditaments rests upon a single *principle*, though a variety of *methods* have been evolved for the application of the principle to some particular classes of hereditament, e.g. industrial undertakings and licensed premises. Put briefly, this principle requires the annual value to be the annual rental which would be paid for the premises in a free market determined by supply and demand. The valuer has to consider what rent the hereditaments would attract in a free market. He is not bound by the rents actually being paid, which may be either more than market rent or less. On the same corollary, the tenant he is to consider is not the actual one but a hypothetical one.

The Annual Value is calculated in two ways. In the assessment of manufactories the Annual Value is directly estimated by reference to the receipts, and is defined to be 'the estimated rent which the hereditament might reasonably be expected to let from year to year if the tenant undertook to pay all tenants' rates and taxes and to bear the cost of repairs and insurance and the other expenses, if any, necessary to maintain the hereditaments in a state to command that rent'. In other hereditaments, including the large class of shops and house-property, the Annual Value is a derivative of a larger figure called Gross Annual Value. This is estimated first on a definition which states that the landlord (not the tenant, as in the former case) bears 'the cost of repairs and insurance and the expenses, if any, necessary to maintain the hereditaments in a state to command that rent'. Certain standardized allowances are then deducted from the Gross Value, as so ascertained, to arrive at the effective figure of the Net Annual Value on which rates are paid. The object of the latter procedure is to place landlords' allowances on a standardized footing where this can conveniently be done, e.g. with houses and shops.

The law relating to valuation has been changed frequently since the war. For dwelling houses built after 1918 the Local Government Act, 1948, introduced a new principle of valuation by reference to cost of construction, and for older dwelling-houses assessment was by reference to rents actually paid for comparable property in the locality in 1939. The Valuation for Rating Act, 1953, repealed the provisions about cost of construction before they had actually come into force, and valuation of all dwelling-houses was based on hypothetical rents in 1939 and certain other factors. The first post-war valuation list came into effect in 1956 and was based on these rules. Its impact on shops, offices and other commercial properties was considerable and Parliament passed another Act in 1957 to grant a temporary remission of one-fifth of the new assessments made on these classes of property. The Local Government Act, 1958, reduced the de-rating of industries and freight-transport hereditaments from 75% to 50%. Thus there have been constant shifts in the distribution of the rate burden between different categories of ratepayers. In the current valuation list, which came into force in 1963, the de-rating of industrial and freight-transport hereditaments was ended (Rating and Valuation Act, 1961). Dwelling-houses, shops and offices were rated also on current values, so there were drastic upward adjustments everywhere in the assessments of residential property. Of course, the rate paid by the residential occupier does not increase *pro rata* with the rise in assessments because the rise in total rateable values, including the greater amounts accruing from industrial premises, should permit broadly equivalent reductions in the level of the rate poundage. But any ratepayer will suffer if his own assessment has risen proportionately more than the average of assessments in his area. The rate burden also tends steadily to increase as local authorities are forced to pass on the rising charges for goods and services which they require. Yet the total *share* of rates paid by householders was virtually unchanged by the 1963 revaluation, although the position varied considerably in different parts of the country. Where the market value of residential property had climbed steeply there was a corresponding sharp increase in assessments, e.g. good-quality flats on the South Coast. In Bournemouth the residential share of total rateable value moved up from 48% to 58%; elsewhere, especially in industrial areas, the residential share actually fell. The 1961 Act empowered the Minister of Housing and Local Government to issue Orders which—subject to parliamentary approval—would authorise reductions in dwelling-house assessments in areas where householders were affected very adversely by the changes. The Minister decided, however, to make no such Orders because the changes in the incidence of the rate burden were not large enough to justify fresh impediments to a uniform valuation.

The rating of nationalized industries presents a special problem; their physical assets are not Crown property but are assessable to rates. Three of them, the railways, the gas industry, and the electricity supply industry have fixed plant obviously not self contained in any rating areas. Special arrangements operate under the Local Government Acts 1948 and 1958 for the ascertainment of the total rateable value of such assets in the areas of the owning Boards and the apportionment of the rate liabilities in respect of them among the Rating Authorities.

MACHINERY OF ASSESSMENT

The Rating and Valuation Act of 1925 established a system of quinquennial valuation of all rateable hereditaments, but provided for the assessment of new hereditaments, and changes in existing assessments, to be effected at any time between the quinquennial valuations. The assessments settled on the quinquennial valuations are embodied in what is called the 'Valuation List', and this is supplemented or corrected from time to time, as 'proposals' for new or altered assessments are dealt with.

Before 1925 the work of valuation and the settlement of assessments had been carried out through the machinery of the Poor Law. The Act of 1925 placed the responsibility for initial valuation in the hands of the Rating Authorities. The settlement of the assessments, i.e. the approval of the draft valuation lists submitted by the Rating Authorities, and of any interim proposals put forward either by the Rating Authority or occupiers, was entrusted to local Assessment Committees, one in each County Borough, and several, each covering an appropriate combination of rating areas, in each County. The functions of the Assessment Committees were quasi-judicial; and the Act established a code of procedure before the Assessment Committees and preserved the existing rights of appeal to the Borough or County Courts of Quarter Sessions, on law or fact, and thence to the Court of Appeal on a question of law. To assist in the promotion of uniformity, the Act established Valuation Committees in each County with power to initiate proposals themselves, and a Central Valuation Committee to watch over uniformities on the national plane.

The Rating and Valuation Act 1925 made a big improvement in preceding arrangements, and much that it introduced, in particular the code of procedure for settling assessments, is retained. It did not, however, result in the measure of uniformity in assessment which was predicted. Much of its failure was due to difficulties in rating law and political issues concerning the assessment of dwelling-houses affected by rent-control. It was nevertheless said that it was wrong in principle to entrust the Rating Authorities with initial valuation, even with the functions of the Assessment and Valuation Committees superimposed; and that a proper degree of uniformity could never be achieved through local agency. The introduction of a new general grant for local government largely designed to compensate for disparate rating resources (see later) made uniformity of assessment more important than ever; and it was decided to meet the situation by transferring valuation from the Rating Authorities to the valuation staff of the Commissioners of Inland Revenue and to establish new machinery for the settlement of assessments.

The changes were implemented by the Local Government Act of 1948 which also introduced the new general grant. In place of the Assessment Committees the Act established local Valuation Courts the members of which are drawn from panels prepared by the County and County Borough Councils, subject to Ministry approval. The County and Central Valuation Committees were not preserved. The appeals which formerly went to Quarter Sessions now lie to the Lands Tribunal established, for this and other purposes by the Lands Tribunal Act 1949.

The Act also provided for the resumption of the quinquennial valuations which had been interrupted by the war. After some delay through the reorganization the first post-war valuation proceeded in 1956 and the next was postponed until 1963.

STATE GRANTS

Broadly speaking, the State began to subsidize certain services conducted by Local Authorities because they were recognized as services which were nationally required but which it was necessary, convenient, or best to conduct through local agency. The Police and Education services have been grant-aided virtually from their beginnings in the nineteenth century and most of the Welfare services came to be so assisted as they developed early in the twentieth.

Until 1929, the Government grants, apart from the special subsidies for municipal housing, which took the form of yearly contributions over a term of years towards each house provided by the local Authority (a type of grant called a unit-grant), were 'percentage grants', i.e. the State paid a percentage of the Local Authority's expenditure under approved headings. For a long time most of these grants were at the rate of 50%, reflecting a conception that, in the agency services which they assisted, the State and the Local Authorities should virtually be, not only partners but equal partners. Today, when the general relationships between State and Local Authority are in many ways different from what they were, and rest, as we shall see, on new methods of regulating them, there seems to be no special virtue in the rate of 50%; and percentage grants, now operating over a curtailed range, may in future be looked at with much more of an eye to the aim and characteristics of the particular service.

The ten years after the close of the first World War were years of violent political controversy over the increased level of public expenditure and of taxation, central and local. The period had been one of growing industrial depression and of unemployment on a scale never before experienced. The Social Services in particular, having steadily grown over many years,

E

as we have seen, came in for sharp attack. The percentage grants to the Local Authorities in respect of them were assailed on the ground that the percentage principle itself encouraged spending by the Local Authorities and left the State with an undefined and largely uncontrollable commitment. In conditions of industrial depression and unemployment the need for Social Services was obviously greater than ever, but it was argued that the consequent high levels of taxation were 'a burden on industry', increasing productive costs so as to handicap export production in particular, and thus setting up a 'vicious circle'.

In comparison with the levels of public expenditure and rates of taxation current in the period following the second World War, those current in 1929 do not appear so staggering as they did then. As for 'the burden on industry' the flourishing state of British industry, of production for export, and the maintenance of full employment since 1945 all seem convincing proof that something other than levels of public expenditure and taxation must have been at the root of all industrial depression of the decade 1920-1930. The truth is that the principle of the Social Services and the Welfare State they built up was neither so generally accepted, nor so widely regarded as inevitable, as it is today. The views we have recited, however were those politically dominant in 1929, and so far as local government was concerned they resulted in the financial provisions of the Local Government Act 1929.

This Act 'assisted agriculture' by removing the 25% liability for rates to which agricultural land and buildings remained subject under previous legislation (thus de-rating them entirely); and afforded 'relief to industry' by de-rating to the extent of 75% 'industrial hereditaments', i.e. those, other than public supply undertakings, in which some process of manufacture is carried on, and 'freight transport undertakings'. It introduced a general or block grant called 'The General Exchequer Contribution' in displacement of a number of percentage grants. It fixed the general grant initially and provided for subsequent adjustments of its level by Parliament so as to allow of fixed grant periods—the first of 3, the second of 4, and those following of 5 years. It did not, therefore, completely 'freeze' the amount of State assistance, but it did, as was intended, put some check on local spending through curtailing the range of percentage grants and by 'freezing' the amount of central aid for the whole of each grant period.

The distribution of the grant (of which payment was to be made to the County Boroughs and Counties and apportioned by the latter among the Boroughs and Districts) was based on an elaborate formula based on 'weighted population' in which the factors for weighting made such adjustment as was then thought possible or desirable for varying levels in financial resources, i.e. rateable value, and service needs arising out of area-characteristics.

In spite of defects, the 1929 Act introduced principles which are now well-established in the financial relationship between State and Local Authority. Firstly, it is recognized that there is a large area of local finance to which a general grant is appropriate, though opinions will no doubt differ from time to time as to whether some particular service falls within that area or should be dealt with by percentage grant. Secondly, it is seen that the general grant can be a medium for dealing with the root-problem of disparity of financial resources among the Local Authorities, particularly in its impact upon the agency services which are virtually national services. The general grant can also, as we shall see, have substantial administrative advantages.

The Act did in fact reveal its defects before very long. Not all the supporters of the Government which introduced the measure had believed very firmly in the virtues of de-rating; and in Local Authority circles the feeling grew that it had no such general benefit as was claimed for it, while it created inequalities among different classes of ratepayers and left a substantial gap in local revenues when new industry settled in, owing to the freezing of the de-rating loss at the 1929 level. The Local Authorities found themselves, in the event, unable to resist the continuing pressures for expanded services, and the effect of the Act in its overall operation was to leave them to bear an increasing proportion of the cost of national services.

No early change in standing arrangements could be expected when war broke out in 1939 and temporary grants became necessary for Civil Defence and other emergency services; but the situation obviously called for attention when the war ended. It was dealt with by the Local Government Act 1948.

This Act substituted, for the Block Grant under the Act of

1929 a new general grant entitled 'The Exchequer Equalization Grant'. This was designed to pay more heed, in a new formula for its distribution, to the root-problem of disparity in resources. The formula provided for making up, to all Local Authorities whose rateable value fell below the national average, the deficiency in revenue so accruing. In effect, the Exchequer became a ratepayer of the poorer Authorities to the extent of their deficiency in rateable value in each case. The specific factor 'rateable-value per head of population' operative in the 1929 formula was not retained, being covered more fully in this new way. The weighting for unemployment relief in the formula of 1929 also disappeared, since the responsibility for the financial relief of unemployment was being removed from the Local Authorities by extensions of national insurance and by the National Assistance Act 1948 establishing the National Assistance Board as the new agency. Weightings for children under 5 and for sparsity of population in county areas were retained.

After some years there was wide agreement that the Act had proved a good 'equalizer' of resources, but had not done very much to provide for inescapable differences of need. It is fair to remember that the burden for unemployment relief had been lifted, and that the Government which introduced the measure was more favourably disposed to percentage grants than the Government of 1929 and may have been relying much more on them to cope with any new needs.

Needs continued, in fact, to grow, and in 1956 a new Government announced that it was reviewing the whole situation and system. Later it produced a White Paper, Cmnd 209 of 1957, entitled *Local Government Finance*. In this the Government rejected some proposals for radical changes in the system of local taxation, e.g. local income-tax and the opening up of other new sources of local revenue, reaffirmed its belief in the rating system, declared its intention to modify de-rating and outlined proposals for a new general grant on revised lines, displacing more percentage grants, notably those for education (but not school milk and meals) the fire service and certain domiciliary health and welfare services.

The measures outlined in the White Paper were embodied in the Local Government Act 1958. The Act in fact introduced two general grants in place of the one Exchequer Equalization

Grant under the Act of 1948,—the one designed as an equalizer, called the Rate Deficiency Grant, paid direct to the Boroughs and District as well as the Counties and County Boroughs and distributed on the same principle of making up deficiencies as that in the grant of 1948; the other, in fact divided into basic and supplementary grants, distributed on a new and greatly elaborated formula designed to take account of needs. Apart from population, dealt with through the basic grant, the weightings for need, in the supplementary grants, are number of school children, number of children under 5, number of old people (over 65), high density or low density of population, declining population, and higher costs in Greater London.

Grant Orders made by the Minister but subject to Parliamentary approval will settle grant over periods of two or three years but not necessarily at the same annual level in each period; and in fixing the annual level regard must be had to the latest information about Local Authority expenditure on the range of services deemed to be assisted (fire, education, health, care of children), probable fluctuations in expenditure which lie beyond local control, the need for development, and the extent to which it is reasonable to develop in general economic conditions. The general grant is payable to Counties and County Boroughs with payment, under certain rules, by the Counties to the Boroughs and Districts.

On this footing the system of general grants has obviously been made much more elastic and responsive, many of the objections which could legitimately be made to it, as introduced in 1929, are no longer valid, the aims sought in distribution have been clarified, the measure in which they are realized will become more visible, and the distribution itself has been effected on much more adequate and equitable lines.

The old problem of disparity in resources has not been entirely eliminated over the whole range of local government functions and services, but its effect has been greatly tempered in many vital sectors and one effect of this should be that local government areas can be shaped with more regard to general and administrative factors.

The Government have also claimed that the changes give wider scope for local autonomy and greater freedom for Local Authorities to establish their own priorities among their services from time to time. Since percentage grants inevitably involve much detailed central control the change could also mean less manpower (at both ends), less paper-work, and less administrative costs. We say 'could' for the services deemed to be assisted remain subject to the powers of promotion and control which we noticed in Chapter III as arising quite irrespective of approvals to grant-aided expenditure. Let us hope they are not exercised so as to re-establish the types of control operative when the services were dealt with through percentage grants.

The latest development in central grants is the Rating (Interim Relief) Act, 1964. This provides for payment of an extra £6,500,000 p.a. to local authorities which is roughly a one per cent addition to the total of Exchequer grants. Distribution of this grant is designed to assist local authorities with a high proportion of elderly persons: the grant is made at the rate of £5 per head in respect of people over 65 years of age where they exceed 10% of the population. As noticed above, this Act also enables a local authority to remit rates in cases of hardship and, since hardship is common among elderly people living on fixed incomes, the idea of the Act is to compensate for the consequent loss of rate income. However, the Act is a very unsatisfactory piece of legislation because there is no guarantee that the extra money will go to those parts of the country that need it most. A grant paid to a local authority benefits all the inhabitants of the area, not merely those who suffer hardship from an increase in rates. There is no evidence whatever that the greatest concentration of poverty is to be found in areas with most old people; poverty is more likely to be widespread in industrial areas with substantial experience of unemployment. The 1964 Act is clearly a temporary measure designed to offset some of the protests caused by rate increases that followed the 1963 revaluation,—increases that were particularly sharp in residential south coast areas to which many people retire. Because of this discontent the Government also appointed a committee under the chairmanship of Professor Allen to undertake a general review of the rating system. When the Allen Committee issues its findings other changes may follow.

BORROWING FOR CAPITAL EXPENDITURE

A Local Authority raises no fund such as the share capital of a company, on which a dividend is paid. But, like any private entrepreneur, it requires sums to equip the enterprise and to augment this equipment if the service expands. These sums must often be larger than any received over short periods of account, whether from the yield of a rate-levy or, in the case of trading undertakings, from the charges made to the consumer. In any event, though no question of annual dividend arises, it is not equitable that the cost of assets which will serve the ratepayers or the consumers over a long period—assets of a capital nature, as book-keepers call them—should be borne out of a levy of rates or charges in a single year. Apart from other objections, ratepayers and consumers change from year to year. As the equipment has to be provided at the outset of the service, the Local Authority raises the money by borrowing on the security of all its revenues, actual and potential. The money so raised is called its capital, or its debt, but it should be appreciated that all of it reflects tangible assets, and that some of it, i.e. that of the trading services, is fully remunerative in a commercial sense.

The municipality's capital, or debt, is obviously of the same character as the loan capital or debentures of a company; but whereas there is nothing to prevent the loan capital of a company, as well as its share capital, from being irredeemable, the capital of the Local Authority must be redeemed within a prescribed period. There are several ways in which the Local Authority arranges for this, but all of them involve a setting aside out of yearly or other periodical revenue from the rates, or from the charges made to consumers, as the case may be, in such measures and fashion as will either discharge the debt by instalments, or redeem it at the end of the period in which the whole debt must be cleared off; while at the same time paying the current interest on the loans effected. In reality, then, *all* the expenditure of the Local Authorities is ultimately defrayed, as was stated at the commencement of this chapter, from its periodical revenues; but in the case of capital expenditure the cost is spread over a comparatively long period of years. The periods within which the loan has to be redeemed are not necessarily coincident with the repayment periods in the transactions of the Local Authority with the lenders, though the latter cannot exceed the former. Much depends on the particular way in which the loans are affected, whether short- or medium-term mortgages, bonds, or long-term stock, etc. Within the total loan period sanctioned, say 60 years, successive loans may be taken up for shorter periods.

Some, but not all, of the assets thus acquired are of a wasting nature, deteriorating in usefulness or value. The maximum periods for the redemption of the loan are therefore related to the anticipated life of the assets bought out of the borrowed money. Some assets, such as land, do not waste and often grow in value. In the eighteenth century, for instance, Liverpool bought land in the centre of the city for a few thousand pounds which was some years ago estimated to be worth £12,000,000. In the case of land and other non-wasting assets, the maximum loan period chosen is largely a matter of convenience and is therefore longer than in other cases. There is, in any event, no need for the municipality to provide in the way that companies do for 'depreciation', as it is called, since the Local Authorities' redemption of capital fulfils an identical function.

If the service continues, and the asset has to be renewed or replaced, the municipality, debt-free in respect of it, can borrow again for the replacement or renewal. In the trading services, however, the Local Authority can often largely avoid such a course; because it may be empowered to accumulate reserve or renewal funds by contributions from periodical revenue over and above the contributions which have to be set aside towards redemption of debt. The effect is obviously to enable the Local Authority to renew its capital assets, such as plant and equipment of all kinds, or to acquire additional ones, without recourse to further borrowing, and thus to save interest charges. Borrowing can also be avoided by purchasing some assets of a capital nature out of current revenues, but if capitalization of this kind were raised to extreme limits, its effect could be unfair on the ratepayers or consumers of a particular year or class. This course, though fairly freely allowed in rate-borne services, and practised wherever reasonably possible by the Local Authorities, has often, therefore, been fairly closely regulated by statute, e.g. particularly in electricity supply before nationalization.

Before 1953 there was no general power to accumulate reserves or renewal funds for capital expenditure on services borne by rates, apart from power to include an amount for contingencies in rate estimates for a particular year. With their experience of the trading undertakings in mind, many Local Authorities moved in recent years towards the view that such a power should be available. The question is a wider one than it may seem; since on ultimate analysis it could raise constitutional questions as to the relation between central and local government, and the relation between the levels of national and local taxation in fiscal policy as a whole. Special local powers were obtained by the Liverpool and Coventry Corporations in their Local Acts of 1930. Each of these established a Capital Reserve Fund, and allowed annual contributions to it from rate revenue not exceeding the equivalent of a rate of twopence in the pound, and from trading surpluses of 1 per cent. of the outstanding debt, but no contribution of the latter kind is to be made unless the Reserve Fund of the contributory undertaking is itself at its statutory maximum. The Coventry Act also authorized the payment into the Fund of the proceeds of the sale of any corporate estate. The Liverpool Act limited the Fund to a quarter of a million pounds, and expenditure out of the Fund to £5,000 for any one transaction. Similar though not quite identical powers were subsequently obtained by other Authorities, the limitations on the Fund varying in the individual cases.

Now however, the Local Government (Miscellaneous Provisions) Act 1953, confers general powers to establish reserve and renewals funds. The levels of both funds are left to ministerial prescription, and yearly contributions to the capital fund are limited to the product of fourpenny, threepenny, and twopenny rates for County Borough, County, and District Councils respectively.

Local Authorities can never borrow without statutory authority to do so. Where borrowing powers are contained in Local Private Acts they are usually limited to prescribed sums; and in both Local and General Acts the powers are now almost invariably given subject to the sanction of the appropriate Ministry to particular loans raised under the powers. As we saw in the last chapter, it is through their jurisdiction over loans that the Ministries exercise one of the most fundamental of central controls. It is they who fix the maximum periods within which the loans are to be redeemed, basing their prescriptions in this respect upon the standard rates, invariably cautious, that are established in the business and accounting world for the depreciation of various classes of asset. No sanction is required for temporary borrowings (mostly effected through bank overdraft) to meet expenses ahead of revenue or pending receipt of loan-sanctions—for which a general power is contained in the Local Government Act of 1933.

To meet conditions arising out of the war, borrowing by Local Authorities in the immediate post-war period was confined to loans from a central Board funded by the State. An arrangement on these lines had been operating for the smaller Local Authorities for many years before 1939; but the larger Local Authorities resorted to the market, and, if they could satisfy certain conditions required for central approval, often had recourse to issues of stock. Nevertheless, a policy of providing loans through an official agency is often supported in local government circles on the grounds of administrative simplicity and that it may provide slightly lower interest rates. The requirement that all borrowing should be undertaken through a Government agency was withdrawn in 1952. Under current national policy Local Authorities satisfy their capital requirements in the open market, through stock issues and mortgage bonds, but the smaller authorities also use the agency, the Public Works Loan Board.

A new arrangement in dealing internally with capital finance is the Loans Pool, which can be introduced by Counties and County Boroughs and, with Ministerial consent, Boroughs and Districts of 60,000 or more. Under this, the average rate of interest on the whole of the Authority's outstanding debt is charged to all the capital projects instead of the rate actually incurred on the borrowing for the particular project. The effect of equating interest charges in this way is claimed to be equitable on the whole, to be helpful in assessing the Authority's overall capital position, and to simplify administration and accounting. Its impact on some services is not invariably equitable, and its effect is to obscure, in some measure, the economic appraisement of the individual services and projects —unless, at any rate, the actual and not the notional interest charges are used in costing.

CHAPTER V

The Local Authority's Constitution

THE ORGANS of English local government are, with one exception, elected Councils. In a Rural Parish certain powers are reserved to the Parish Meeting even when a Parish Council is established; so that where there is no Parish Council the Local Authority is in effect the Parish Meeting, and where there is a Parish Council, the Meeting is the Local Authority for some purposes, the Council for others. Otherwise, the Local Authorities of England are the County Councils, the County Borough Councils, the Borough Councils, the Urban District Councils, and the Rural District Councils.

All these Councils may appoint committees; and they possess considerable freedom to establish whatever organization they think best in order to discharge their responsibilities, and to appoint the agencies and instruments through which they will do so. It is important to remember, however, that the English system does not provide for any kind of separate executive body with power of its own, formed out of, or working side by side with, the elected Council; and that the elected Council remains politically and legally responsible for the acts of its agents and instruments such as its committees and officers.

In order to make this responsibility effectual, and at the same time to enable the Local Authority to conduct its business and manage its property effectively under our legal system, the Local Authority is generally incorporated. It becomes what is known to the law as a 'corporation', or 'body corporate'—an artificial person having continuity of life, a continuing identity, notwithstanding changes in its component personnel, and the power to hold property as though it were an individual. In Boroughs it is the Mayor, the Aldermen, and the 'burgesses' at large, including (though they are not specially named) the Councillors, who are theoretically incorporated; but as the local government statutes provide that the powers of the corporation are to be exercised by the Council, the effect in practice is the same as if the Council itself had been incorporated, as in fact is the case with County Councils, District Councils, and Parish Councils. All the Councils except Parish Councils have a Common Seal. In a Parish where there is no Parish Council, the body corporate (in whom the parish property is vested) is the Chairman of the Parish Meeting, together with the Councillor representing the Parish on the Rural District Council, these being styled 'the representative body of the Parish.'

COUNCILLORS

The composition of the Councils differs according to the type of Local Authority, but the main element in all of them is a body of Councillors directly elected at the polls for a term of three years. In the Counties, the Metropolitan Boroughs, and the Rural Parishes, these Councillors retire *en bloc* every three years. In the Boroughs (County or Non-County) one-third of them (one out of three in each Ward) retire each year, so that here the elections are annual and not triennial. In Urban and Rural Districts the standing arrangement is the same as in the Boroughs, but by a two-thirds majority, and with the consent of the County Council, Urban and Rural Councils may change to the system of retirement *en bloc* with a triennial election. In the Boroughs and the Districts there has always been much controversy as to which of the two arrangements is the better. Annual elections ensure a quicker response on the part of the Local Authority to changing currents of opinion and new needs, while at the same time ensuring a nucleus of experienced councillors from year to year continuously; but from a purely administrative point of view the annual upheaval of an election involving a third of the number of Councillors sometimes proves a drawback, since it is bound in some measure to disturb or delay the Council's business. In the case of the Counties there is no option in law. Nor would it be practicable to hold the elections there annually. The electoral divisions in the Boroughs, known as Wards, are so arranged that three Councillors can sit for each, and one of them can retire annually; but in the Counties there is only one Councillor's seat in each electoral division, because the electoral divisions of the County are of necessity so large that the numbers on the County

Council would be of unmanageable proportions if three seats were allotted to each division. Before 1949, the constitutional year of a Borough ran from 9th November, the date of the Annual Meeting, the elections taking place on the 1st November. The constitutional year of the Districts ran from 15th April, and of the Counties from 16th March, after elections held just before. But the Representation of the People Act 1948 fixed the one season of the year for the elections and Annual Meetings of all Authorities—April for the County Councils and May for the others.

Prior to 1945, the local government franchise was restricted to those who occupied land or unfurnished premises, or whose wives or husbands did; but today it is based on residence. Broadly speaking, all British subjects not expressly disqualified by Statute, and over the age of 21 years, male or female, have a vote if they have been placed upon the Register of Voters as residing within the area on a qualifying date, or as occupying as owner or tenant any rateable land or premises in the area of the yearly value of not less than ten pounds. The arrangements are such as to preclude an elector from exercising more than one vote in the same election.

Qualifications for candidature as a Councillor at one time varied according to the type of Authority, but are now uniform. The candidates must be of full age and British subjects, and if these requirements are both satisfied, they may then claim qualification on any of three grounds, namely, that they are on the Register of Local Government Electors for the area, that they own freehold or leasehold land within the area (without limitation of value), or that they have resided in the area for the whole twelve months preceding the day of election. Disqualifications are likewise now uniform, and may accrue in three ways, namely, lack of the positive qualifications (but it does not follow that the seat is vacant if the qualification fails during the Councillor's term of office); failure to attend meetings during a period of six months, unless the reasons therefore have been approved by the Local Authority; and certain positive statutory disqualifications. The latter are as follows: (a) the holding of any paid office or other place of profit under the Council or any of their committees; (b) adjudication as a bankrupt, or the making of a composition or arrangement with creditors; (c) being or having been surcharged by a District

Auditor to an amount exceeding £500 since election or within five years before the day of election; (d) being convicted of an offence since election or within five years of the day of election and sentenced to imprisonment for not less than three months without option of a fine; and (e) disqualification under any enactment relating to corrupt or illegal practices at elections. A person having contracts with the Local Authority is not disqualified; nor indeed is he prevented, if elected as a Councillor, from entering into contracts with the Local Authority; but he must during his membership conform to certain statutory directions to declare his interest and refrain from discussion and voting upon the contract or other matter in which he has a direct or indirect pecuniary interest.

A Parish Council used to be elected by a show of hands at the annual Parish Meeting, or by poll if then demanded, but this method was abolished by the Representation of the People Act 1948. Today all local government elections are held by secret ballot, and under elaborate statutory codes. For the purposes of representation and the election of members, the areas of all Local Authorities are, or can be, divided into electoral divisions, which divisions in the case of a Borough are known as Wards. An administrative County *must* be divided into such electoral divisions, and, as already mentioned, no electoral division of a County can be represented by more than one County Councillor. A Borough, whether County or Non-County, need not be divided into Wards; but almost invariably is. On all grants of new Charters, the Ministries and the Privy Council require a division into Wards, and this is arranged for in the Charter of Incorporation. To provide for the system of annual retirement in rotation, three Councillors' seats are normally allotted to each Ward, but sometimes there are anomalous or transitional arrangements by which a Ward may have six seats, two of which become vacant each year in rotation. Naturally enough, it becomes necessary from time to time to adjust the boundaries, and even the number, of Wards (involving in the latter case an adjustment of the total numbers of the Council). The alterations are effected in the case of a County Council by the Home Secretary, and in the case of a Borough by an Order in Council approving a scheme prepared by a Commissioner appointed by the Home Secretary. For fixing or altering the electoral divisions of a Rural District powers are vested in the

County Council; but the powers are only to be exercised as incidental to fixing or altering the number of Rural District Councillors. The divisions into which the Rural District is divided may be either Parishes, or combinations of parishes, or Wards of Parishes. The County Council has likewise power to fix or alter Wards in an Urban District and to alter the number of Councillors, whether incidentally to fixing or altering Wards or otherwise. The proposals may be initiated by the County Council or the Urban District Council. Unlike a Rural District Council, an Urban District Council has rights of appeal to the Home Secretary if the County Council refuse to act or to make an order; and the Home Secretary—though his confirmation is not required to any Order the County Council do make—may himself make any Order that the County Council might have made. Machinery is available to make adjustments of Wards, etc., following upon changes in status and boundaries. It should be noted that the Wards of a Borough are designed for electoral and representative purposes only and have no administrative significance.

ALDERMEN

In the administrative Counties, and in the County and Non-County Boroughs, a part of the whole Council, numbering one to every three Councillors, consists of a body of Aldermen. Thus, in a Borough of 7 Wards, where the normal arrangement of 3 Councillors to a Ward is operative, and the number of Councillors would number 21, there would in addition be 7 Aldermen, raising the number of the entire Council to 28. In the Greater London Council and the London Boroughs the proportion of Aldermen is a sixth. The Aldermen are elected by, but not necessarily from among, the Councillors. In other words, they stand for election not at the polls by the electors, but are all chosen at certain meetings of the Council by the Councillors. They hold office for six years, twice the term of a Councillor; and matters are so arranged that half, or as nearly half as possible, retire together half-way through the term of office of the others; so that the election of Aldermen recurs at three-yearly intervals.

The elections take place at the Annual Meeting of the Council in the year in which an election of Aldermen is due.

The Councillors vote by a written and signed vote naming the person they wish to see elected; and their votes must be individually recorded in the minutes of the meeting.

Most ordinary decisions of a Council are by a majority of those present and voting, and this means that where the decision is one of appointment, and several names are voted upon, it is not enough that one of the candidates should secure a higher number of votes than the others; he must secure more votes than all the others put together, for otherwise there is no majority of those present and voting in his favour. But legislation provides that in an election of Aldermen the person elected is the nominee receiving the highest number of votes. Usually Aldermen are chosen from among the Councillors, in which case a by-election for new Councillors must follow, whether it is a casual vacancy in the office of Alderman that is being filled or whether the occasion be the periodic election caused through the retirement of half the total number. An Alderman may be elected from among persons *qualified to be* Councillors; but, for reasons into which we need not enter here, Councils seldom resort to the power they have to choose such persons 'from outside' their own ranks.

Neither individually nor collectively, neither in law nor in practice, have Aldermen any special rôle in administration. They have no special privileges or powers; and save in one particular they do not even possess any special or additional duties. In Boroughs they act as Returning Officers at the election of the Councillors, but only if the Borough is divided into Wards; and at each Annual Meeting the Council will appoint an Alderman so to act for each Ward during any election in the ensuing municipal year, including the annual elections which will occur just before its expiry. The duties of a Returning Officer are concerned, not with the electoral poll, but with the subsequent count of the votes, the Returning Officer presiding as a sort of Chairman, adjudicating on doubtful votes, and deciding by lot if there is an equality of votes. But most if not all of these duties are in the Counties and Districts left to the Clerk of the Local Authority, and even in a Borough it is customary for the Returning Officer to discharge the functions of his office with the advice of the Town Clerk; so that even in Boroughs the special duties of an Alderman are not extensive.

The fact that the office is not one of great consequence, but is one of unquestioned prestige, strengthens, if anything, the considerable body of criticism which it has attracted on grounds of principle. It confers an immunity from the rough-and-tumble of the polls for a fairly long period, and this, taken in conjunction with the fact that it is filled by indirect election, stamps it as undemocratic. The system seems to have been introduced by the Municipal Corporations Act 1835 as a link with the past of the ancient chartered corporations, of which Aldermen were an organic part, and as an element which could secure some continuity of policy and personnel. Where triennial elections are held and the whole body of Councillors may be rejected at the polls, the system may have value. Such an argument cannot apply in the Boroughs where elections are annual.

Aldermen are selected by a variety of criteria. Occasionally the choice is made on purely personal grounds; more often it is based either on seniority or party politics. Where politics dominate the loyalties of council members, aldermanic elections will be settled in a party context: either the majority party will take all, or nearly all, the aldermanic seats, or the parties may come to an agreement to share aldermen proportionately with the number of their councillors. Local arrangements between party groups sometimes break down, and this creates much ill-feeling. Indeed, whatever method of selection is in vogue, an aldermanic election may stimulate personal tension among the members of a local authority,—a situation that is not conducive to harmonious concentration upon the essential tasks of local administration. It is not surprising that criticism of the aldermanic system has been common in recent years especially as, due to the growth of the party element in local elections, it can be used in the Boroughs to frustrate the will of the electorate. Since aldermanic elections are held every third year, a party that gains a sweeping victory in a non-aldermanic year can obtain no extra aldermen even if a council follows the convention of allocating aldermen between party groups *pro rata* with their councillors. Thus Party A might have a majority of popularly elected councillors while Party B retains an overall majority of council seats through its aldermen. It is even possible in an aldermanic election year for a party with one fewer councillors than its opponents to retain control provided that it has a majority of non-retiring alder-

F

men. The technique works in this way. As non-retiring aldermen may vote in the election of Mayor or County Council Chairman, a party can use these votes to secure the election of one of its own aldermen as Mayor or Chairman. In the following election of aldermen, the occupant of the Chair is entitled to vote; he uses his vote to force a tie, thereupon he uses his casting vote to secure the aldermanic seats for his party colleagues. This blatant abuse, which is entirely legal, has occurred on a few occasions. It certainly adds weight to the case for the abolition of aldermen. The case in their favour is essentially that they assist councils by giving continuity of experience, but this advantage scarcely outweighs the demerits of an undemocratic process, the possibility of party manipulation and of senile influence in public affairs.

COUNCIL CHAIRMEN AND MAYORS

All Councils are required by law to elect someone who will preside over their meetings during the ensuing constitutional year. The person so chosen is called a Chairman, except in a Borough, where he is called a Mayor, and fulfils, by tradition if not law, a function considerably wider than a Chairman's. As in the case of Aldermen, a Chairman need not be chosen from among the members of the Council but may be chosen 'from outside' the Council's ranks from persons *qualified to be* Councillors. In Counties and Boroughs, Aldermen due to retire do not participate in the election of Chairman or Mayor (which is always the first business at an Annual Meeting; the Aldermanic elections, if any, following). Otherwise the selection is made by an ordinary vote of the Council, in which Aldermen and Councillors alike participate.

The exact rôle of the Mayor of a Borough or County Borough, including a Mayor who has the style of Lord Mayor (a style usually confined to Mayors of cities but not conferred on all of these), is not one which is easily understood by the citizens among whom he must move. The office is one thing by law, and another thing—usually a much bigger thing—by custom. The office is one of long tradition, high prestige, and wide scope for good influence; but whatever a Mayor does he must do by the prestige of his office and by the personal influence he exercises in it, for he is clothed with little legal authority. Apart from his duties as Chairman in presiding over the Council and ordering its procedure and debates according to the Council's Standing Orders, the Mayor of an English Borough has no special rôle to fulfil in the discharge of the municipality's work or in its administration. A Mayor in America, in towns where the Mayor-and-Council system of government has not been displaced by the Commission or Council-and-Manager system, is like the President of the United States in relation to Congress, a Chief of the Executive or Administration, with powers of his own, independent of the elected Council. A French Mayor is in a similar position, and is also for many purposes, an officer of the central government. Much the same is true of the Burgomaster in the countries of western and northern Europe. But an English Mayor is none of these things; and has few powers of his own, apart from those of a Chairman. If the Borough is not divided into Wards he will act as Returning Officer at the elections for the Borough. He has, as Mayor, certain powers in the arrangements for the polls. Surprising as it may be, the Mayor's powers extend no further.

By custom and tradition, however, the Mayor is looked upon as the town's civic leader and chief citizen. He is, in fact, given by statute 'precedence in all places in the Borough', except over a direct representative of the Crown such as the Lord-Lieutenant of the County. His main function is to promote and express the town's civic sense; to represent the Council to the town, and if necessary the town to the Council; and to personify the town to distinguished visitors and the world outside it. To these ends it is essential that he moves freely and frequently among all classes of the community. This indeed becomes the activity which occupies most of his time, and in the substantial towns it is recognized that to fulfil these 'outside duties' he must during his year of office abandon much of his ordinary work as a member of the Council, if he is one. If he is engaged in local politics, whether as a member of the Council or otherwise, he is expected to refrain from any active participation in them during his year of office, and indeed to suspend for the time being his contacts with his local party organization.

It must not be supposed, however, that the influence and prestige of a Mayor are valuable only in outside duties. They can be invaluable in the Council's own sphere of policy and administration; but, if they are to be and remain valuable, it is imperative that the occasions on which they are either solicited or exercised should be the appropriate ones. In general it is not for the Mayor to concern himself with the Local Authority's administration. He cannot direct its officers, for they are responsible to the Council only through the appropriate Committees. And since, as we shall see, the proper channels of administration are the Committees, it is the Chairmen of these Committees who primarily keep in touch with, and are consulted by, the Officers on the Council's business. A Mayor should therefore be careful not to double the rôle of a Committee Chairman. There are, however, occasions and issues, in which general public sentiment may be engaged, which should properly come under the Mayor's notice, and on which therefore he should be consulted by the Officers or the Chairman of the Committee whose functions are concerned. Again, in the best-ordered organizations occasions arise for mediation in domestic counsels, and the Mayor is obviously the proper person to fulfil such a function. Much of the effectuality of the Mayor's influence on occasions of both kinds will depend upon the fact that it is generally held in reserve and exercised sparingly. Much of his influence, within the Council as well as outside it, depends too upon his standing above the dust of Council controversy; and it is with this latter consideration in mind that many Councils provide by Standing Order that the Mayor shall not be Chairman of a Standing Committee during his year of office. The Town Clerk being usually the Mayor's adviser as well as the Council's principal officer, it is best that the Mayor's interest or mediation should be solicited through him, whether by Departmental Heads or Chairmen of Committees.

Legislation allows the remuneration of a Chairman of a County or District Council and a Mayor. The allowance is often called a salary. It is rightly so called in that the recipients are not called upon to show how it was spent. It is primarily and usually allowed for the out-of-pocket expenses of their activities, and for the traditional hospitality and charitable gifts they are expected to dispense. The Local Authority also provide secretarial staff, usually as a section of the Town Clerk's Department.

The Mayor may, by writing, appoint a Deputy Mayor—who

will hold office as long as he does, i.e. until his own successor is qualified to act. In authorities other than Boroughs a Deputy Chairman can be elected by the Council. The two offices are not, however, the same—even legally. A Deputy Mayor does not automatically preside over the Council if the Mayor be absent. Indeed, the Council is directed to choose a temporary Chairman and to look for him first from among the Aldermen present, and the Deputy Mayor may not be an Alderman. The statutory provisions relating to a Deputy Mayor seem only explicable on the assumption that their real object is to provide an assistant, or in case of illness a substitute, for the Mayor in his 'outside' duties; and that it is therefore better to leave the choice to him so that he can be assured of someone 'who will work with him'. The provision that he shall appoint a member of the Council if he appoints at all ensures that he shall appoint someone known to them; but it was apparently felt that no one personally nominated by the Mayor should be given the right to preside over the Council. Another reason for not leaving the choice of a Deputy Mayor to the Council may be to keep the choice of the next Mayor open, or free to be dealt with according to local custom, if any, untrammelled by any implication that in choosing a Deputy Mayor the Council were grooming a person for the principal office. But the statutory provisions are capable of several implications, and their bearing upon local conditions can produce many different reactions. It cannot be said that they have everywhere proved very acceptable; though some Councils appear to have settled down quite comfortably to a convention that each Mayor shall appoint his predecessor as his Deputy.

STATUTORY OFFICERS

Officers and servants of the Local Authority do not form an element in its constitution, or of the corporation which is its legal embodiment. Certain high officers are, however, immemorially associated with English civic government, and modern legislation, while giving a general power to Local Authorities to engage such staff as is reasonably necessary for their purpose, specifically directs the appointment of these and other officers. Thus all Local Authorities (except a Parish Council) must appoint a Clerk (called a Town Clerk in a

Borough), a Treasurer, and a Medical Officer of Health. All of these except a Rural District Council must also appoint a Surveyor; and all except a County a Public Health Inspector. No one person may be both Clerk and Treasurer. A Police Authority must appoint a Chief Constable; an Education Authority a Chief Education Officer; and the Counties and County Boroughs, as Authorities under the Children Act 1948, a Children's Officer. But there are in practice many other chief officers which the larger Local Authorities find it necessary to appoint.

There is surprisingly little statutory prescription of the duties of any of the officers—a situation all to the good since it allows elasticity and adjustment and adaptation to changing conditions.

The Clerk or Town Clerk is regarded as the principal officer, and the Royal Commission of 1928 on Local Government supported the view that this recognition should continue. In recent years the Local Authority Associations have agreed to style the Clerk as Chief Administrative and Executive Officer.

The Clerk or Town Clerk is of necessity responsible for the secretarial work of the Council and its Committees. He is usually also the legal officer of the Local Authority. In varying measure he may also be charged with a general oversight of the Council's administration as a whole, and be required to advise upon administrative arrangements, without interfering with the executive functions of other Departmental Heads, in order to secure co-ordination and, where necessary, uniformity of administrative practice. In addition, he is usually looked upon as the Council's chief adviser on questions of policy. The legislation requires a Local Authority to appoint 'a fit person' but does not specify the qualifications. Almost universally, however, Local Authorities appoint solicitors with administrative experience. It will be seen that the Clerk's duties are, or can be, comprehensive in scope; but it should not be supposed that he is in the position of a Managing Director, in an industrial or commercial company, either in relation to the Council or to the other chief officers, such an arrangement being in fact precluded by the statutory direction to appoint other officers, and by legal or other considerations which give them much independent responsibility to the Council for the duties of their respective offices.

The Treasurer is now usually the Council's Chief Financial Officer and Accountant, but in some of the District Authorities an arrangement has been in vogue in the past whereby a Bank Manager has been appointed Treasurer and a separate salaried whole-time Accountant appointed. It is illegal for a Bank, as such, to be appointed a Treasurer, but many Banks are prepared to agree to the appointment of a local Manager as the Local Authority's Treasurer. This practice also allows of an arrangement, not infrequently followed in the past in the smaller Districts, of letting the Clerk be also the Accountant or Chief Financial Officer. The arrangement is disappearing, as there has been wide dissatisfaction with it. It is only possible through making a distinction between the Treasurer and the Accountant under which the Treasurer has the bare statutory responsibilities associated with the custody of the Borough Fund while the Accountant performs the material duties of accountant, collector, and financial adviser. Real responsibility for the vital financial duties is bound to fall upon the Accountant. It may be doubted, therefore, whether the safeguards intended to be provided by the statutory division of the office of Treasurer and Clerk are in fact secured; though the arrangement is disappearing for other administrative reasons we need not mention here. In a well-regulated Local Authority we may assume that the Treasurer is the chief accountant to the Local Authority, its receiver and paymaster, and its financial adviser. Where money is borrowed by stocks and bonds he may be registrar, and until recently he was usually the Authority's valuer for rating.

The office of the Surveyor, though of vital importance, needs no special notice from a constitutional standpoint. The Surveyor is also the Authority's civil engineer and sometimes its architect, and in some towns he is also Water Engineer. In the medium-sized authority the duties of the office are obviously of a very mixed and comprehensive character. In the largest cities or counties, however, the growth of work has necessitated a division of the usual duties of the office, the Authority appointing a Surveyor, Engineer, and Architect. Separate Water Engineers often become desirable at a lower level of size and population.

The office of Public Health Inspector is one which possesses some independent responsibilities, placed by legislation upon this office by name, but legislation also requires the Inspectors to work under the general direction of the Medical Officer of Health. It is this latter Officer who is the head of the Local Authority's health services and who also maintains a general watch over the sanitary conditions of the area.

In general, Local Government Officers hold office during the pleasure of the employing Council, subject to any period of notice which may have been arranged for between the parties and which both may be bound to observe under the general law of master and servant. Some Officers are so exposed, however, to interested opposition through the nature of their duties that Parliament for this reason has imposed the requirement of Ministerial consent to their dismissal. Thus, consent to dismissal is requisite in the case of the Clerk and the Medical Officer of a County, the Medical Officer and Public Health Inspectors of Boroughs and Districts and Chief Constables. The legislation governing the subject has been piecemeal and remains anomalous; but neither the Local Authorities nor their Officers have hitherto shown any strong sign that they desire a further measure of central control. Public conscience, and the strength of Local Government Trade Unionism, have provided some measure of protection, and the growth in the scope and influence of Whitley machinery and practice which has been a feature of recent years holds out the promise that the difficult problems involved in security of tenure may be resolved without resort to central control. In any event, the situation of an Officer threatened with dismissal, but remaining at his post through central intervention, would become exceedingly difficult.

Ministerial control is also used in a few cases as a safeguard against undesirable appointments. The Minister of Education has a veto power over the selection of a Chief Education Officer and the Home Secretary has a similar power over the post of Children's Officer. In addition, the Home Secretary must approve the nomination of Chief Constables; recently this approval has been withheld in a few instances where it was proposed to fill a vacancy by promotion from within the local police force.

BOROUGH AUDITORS

In Boroughs in which the Council has adopted neither professional nor Government audit, the audit of the municipal accounts is conducted by Borough Auditors. These are honorary officers who are not required to have professional experience or qualifications in accountancy. Two of them, known as Elective Auditors, are directly elected in March each year by the local government electors from among persons qualified to be Councillors but who must be neither members nor officers of the Council. The degree of interest in their election is usually infinitesimal. The third Auditor, called the Mayor's Auditor, is appointed by the Mayor from among the members of the Council. As already mentioned, the system is an ineffectual relic of the municipal past, and has largely disappeared.

Whether the audit of accounts be governmental, professional, or elective, it is standard practice in all save the smaller Authorities for the Treasurer or Chief Financial Officer also to maintain a system of *internal* audit with qualified staff.

CHAPTER VI

The Pattern of Administration

As we have seen, central control over local government is considerable, but it has stopped short, for the most part, of the Local Authority's internal organization, and left the Local Authority a wide degree of freedom to choose the means and methods by which it will do its work. However highly developed the Local Authority's machinery may be—and in the case of the larger Authorities it is very highly developed indeed—it rests primarily upon the establishment of committees and the appointment of officers and staff. Generally speaking, such legislative provisions as do concern themselves with the Local Authority's machinery confine themselves to these two essentials. There are, as we have already noted, certain officers whom the Local Authority is bound to appoint. There are likewise some committees which it must appoint, either for a particular service or for a particular aspect of its administration. Prescriptions of this kind, however, are the exception rather than the rule, and the Local Authority is largely free to appoint what officers and committees it likes. That the Local Authorities have been thus free to manage their own households has been, on the whole, a good thing. It has left their arrangements flexible, and responsive to changing times and varying local conditions.

The work of a local authority is based on the inter-relationships of officials and elected representatives working together through a committee system. But, especially in the larger authorities, this pattern is substantially affected by the political loyalties of the elected representatives. It is unrealistic and misleading to ignore the effect of politics on local government, so a broad description of the political setting must be given before we move on to consider the respective rôles of officers and councillors.

THE IMPACT OF POLITICS

It is often argued that politics should have no place in local government. Certainly, there are some grounds for this view. Where elections are held on a party basis, no candidate other than those sponsored by a party, has a real chance of success. Where one party is dominant in a particular ward or district, nomination by that party is tantamount to election to the local council, for electors become accustomed to voting on party lines and do not know, or do not care about, the qualities of the individual candidate. Attachment to a political party thus becomes an essential pre-condition of election to a local council; in so far as this limits the field of recruitment, the quality of elected members may be reduced. There must be many men and women of high ability, who would be willing to serve on local authorities, but who are unwilling to give unswerving support to a party or who happen to belong to a political minority in their own locality. The other main causes of complaint are that where councillors and aldermen organise themselves into political groups, decisions are taken by the majority group in private meetings, and that politics are allowed to affect details of local administration which are quite beyond the normal bounds of party controversy.

Equally, however, a strong case can be made in favour of party politics. Party activity does much to increase interest in local elections: party conflict tends to reduce the number of unopposed elections, and to raise the proportion of the electorate who vote in contested elections. Further, if a candidate is returned unopposed without a party label, it does not follow that he has no political affiliations but merely that he has not declared any he may have. To argue that politics should be taken out of local government is, in part, to misunderstand the nature of politics. In a democracy we argue freely about the proper aims and methods of public policy. This is political discussion. Inevitably, the major questions which confront local authorities, education, housing, planning, raise issues which are political in nature and attract the attention of political organisations. The idea that these matters should be left to 'the best man for the job' is fanciful since one cannot decide who is the best man unless the opinions of candidates are revealed.

The charge that party groups should not have private 'caucas' meetings to settle policy is countered by showing that this is analogous to what happens in our national government; no-one suggests it is wrong for Conservative and Labour M.P.s to hold separate private gatherings or that party leaders should not meet in conditions of secrecy at Cabinet or 'Shadow' Cabinet meetings. Party organisation in a democracy is essential for opinions to be organised into broad streams. The group or party representing the dominant stream of opinion becomes responsible for the conduct of public affairs for a limited time, and may be displaced from power at a subsequent election if it displeases the voters. It follows that where the business of a local authority is conducted on a party basis, the policy of the authority is more likely to be planned and consistent than if it depends on unorganised and changing views of individual councillors.

Whatever view one takes of these theoretical considerations, it is vital to recognise that the impact of politics on local government is growing steadily. Except in rural areas, most local elections are now fought on a party basis. What does vary, however, and what is most difficult to determine, is how far party organisation affects the actual working of a local council. The variety of local arrangements is best illustrated by the description of extremes. In some councils, party loyalty matters little; members are elected on a party basis but, once elected, tend to act as individuals; committee chairmen and aldermen are chosen irrespective of politics and no group meetings are held. This is often the pattern in small towns and in non-industrial areas. At the other extreme, party governs everything important. The majority group meets to determine policy on major issues; it secures a majority on all committees; it nominates the chairmen and vice-chairmen of all committees; either it dominates the aldermanic seats completely or, more likely, by agreement between parties, the aldermen are shared in proportion to the number of their councillors; the parties require complete obedience from their members, and any councillor who refuses to support a party decision is expelled from the group and will not get party support at the next election. Such extensive party influence is common in large towns and other authorities dominated by the Labour Party. There are, of course, many authorities which fall in between the patterns defined above, where party groups meet irregularly or committee chairmanships are not always distributed on a party basis. And sometimes where party loyalties are strong, the effect of politics is restricted because no group has an overall majority of seats.

Against this background of an uneven degree of party activity, the work of local officials and council committees must be considered. Clearly, the officials will have less influence on the direction of local affairs if vital decisions are taken at private 'caucas' meetings which they do not attend. Equally, where party loyalty and discipline are strong, discussion at council committee meetings may be less important. Even so, the picture must not be exaggerated. However intense party activity may be, a mass of minor administrative details are decided by committee debate and by consultation between chief officials and committee-chairmen.

THE RÔLE OF THE OFFICERS

It is manifest from what was said in Chapter I that the administrative, executive, and managerial aspects of the Local Authority's tasks must inevitably be discharged, in modern times, by paid officers and servants who have acquired, in their several ways, the necessary training qualifications, and experience for the expert work involved. This circumstance sets up a relation between officers and the employing Council which is not dissimilar to that which exists in other spheres of administration, whether industrial, commercial, or public. The paid servants actually carry out the work and transact the business for which the Local Authority is responsible, while the Local Authority decides and controls policy (within the limited meaning which that term has in local, as distinct from national, government), and holds the purse-strings.

As in other spheres, this analysis, though sound and real enough if one is thinking in constitutional terms, really oversimplifies the position. The tasks of administration in a modern society (and this is true of any kind of administration) are so complex that high executive officers cannot be confined merely to the rôle of executants of a policy solely initiated by the part-time amateurs who employ them, and who, in local government, are elected at the polls (a description which implies not a jot of disrespect). Nor is it desirable that officers should be confined to such a rôle. As the late Lord Stamp said in his Inaugural Presidential Address to the Institute of Public Administration in 1938: 'The official must be the mainspring of the new society; suggesting, promoting, advising, at every stage. The time when the amateur control is all-wise for either seeing or saying what ought to be done, and the official's job is merely to do what he is told, is now completely past . . . . Only the skilled and trained official can really be relied upon to keep continuity, system, impartial interpretation, tradition, and disinterested impetus.' Lord Stamp's opinion may hold 'errors of emphasis', as the theologians say, but no one who knows local government from the inside, whether he be councillor or officer, will consider it wide of the mark. From a different standpoint Professor Laski has said much the same thing: 'Anyone who has seen an English municipal body at work will have realized that the whole difference between efficient and inefficient administration lies in the creative use of officials by elected persons' (*Grammar of Politics*, page 425).

There is, indeed, a wide recognition in the world of local government of the officers' right to advise on policy. In the most progressive Local Authorities, the officers are expected, and given to understand that they are expected, to do this. It is obviously only the officer, spending his daily life at the centre of the Local Authority's activities, who can measure the impact of the Local Authority's existing policies; who can know the resources of the Local Authority so intimately as to be able to measure their adequacy in conditions of change and growth; whose knowledge of the services is so close, and whose experience so well bedded down, as to make foresight possible; whose conspectus of needs can lead to long-term policies, in which the many-sided requirements of a place are brought into balance and proportion.

All this is not to say that the expert's view is invariably right. It is in fact one of the virtues of the local government administrative system, as distinct from many others, that it provides so many opportunities for testing the expert's advice and discussing it with him, for correcting his tendency to be obsessed by questions of technique, and for examining his conception of means in the clearer perspective of ends so often possessed by the intelligent layman.

Nor does anything we have said or quoted imply that the Local Authority which welcomes advice on policy from its officers, or accords them a large degree of initiative, relinquishes its own control. Local Government Officers are not unaccustomed to having their more ambitious policies rejected, and it belongs to their professional code of conduct to apply a policy with which they may personally disagree as loyally as if it were their own. Against the type of critic who alleges that energetic officers, jealous for the efficiency of 'their' services, ambitious for the progress of these services, and whose advice carries the weight of high ability, are a menace to democratic government because of their influence over policy, it may be urged that it is precisely officers of this kind who usually elaborate in the most effective way the instruments by which the Council is enabled to exercise its essential controls over both administration and policy. It is, for example, able Town Clerks who have worked out most elaborately and effectively the Standing Orders which secure a Council's control over its committees and its departments. It was able Town Clerks and Treasurers who jointly perfected the rudimentary system of budgetary and financial control; and it was able Treasurers who demonstrated the virtues of costing systems as instruments of management for both committees and departmental heads, and perfected the systems in vogue.

The rôle of the officers cannot, however, be fully explained unless we consider their relations with the Councils' committees and not merely with the Council—but first we must discuss the committees from a wider standpoint.

THE RÔLE OF THE COMMITTEES

Even were the formulation of policy not a conjoint effort of elected representatives and officers, as it is, the Council would be too large a body to perform such a function satisfactorily. Councillors are people with livelihoods to earn and only limited time to spare, and the time has long passed when in even the smallest Authority, the matters to be considered can be dealt with by full meetings of the Council, even if these were held every day or two. Again, the very fact that the Council must concern itself with important issues of policy is, or ought to be, a factor justifying the allocation to some smaller body of work of minor importance. At meetings of the full Council, held in public, it is the debate on policy and principle which should occupy the limited time available; and there is much detailed work which can safely be left to a committee. Again, even large questions are better sorted out by a smaller number. For the formulation, as distinct from the settlement, of policy the workmanlike atmosphere of the committee-room is better than the atmosphere of public debate. It is when questions of policy have crystallized into proposals, and when these are put forward as a coherent whole, that the time arrives for public debate in full Council. Still another consideration is the desirability of affording each branch of the Council's work a measure of continuous and concentrated interest and attention.

Added to all these reasons, however, is the feeling that the elected representatives need to work in close concert with their officers, both in the field of policy and administration, and that the only effective way to secure this is through the committees. It is the close contact between committee and departmental head that renders the supervision of officers by the elected representatives so much more effective in local government than in other spheres. This is not, however, the only, or even the supreme, virtue of this close contact. It also enables the officer proposing policy to discuss it, in the right atmosphere, with the committee whose work is affected by it, before it is placed before the Council. The supervision of administration is thus coupled with a process in which policy is evolved through the intimate collaboration of experts and public representatives, each side educating the other by the frankest and fullest interchange of opinion and information, and by mutual criticism and suggestion.

Summarizing, we may say that the rôle of committees is three-fold, namely, (1) to exercise supervision on the Council's behalf over the departments; (2) in collaboration with the officers to advise the Council on policy and to prepare detailed measures of policy for the Council's consideration; and (3) in some measure to exercise the Council's own powers in matters of less importance. These varying functions are so comprehensive, and so closely associated, that the flow of business through committees scours deep administrative channels from which few items can safely be diverted. When a committee is established to concern itself with a particular branch of business, all matters arising from the Council's decision in that field of business should first be considered by the committee.

THE RELATIONS BETWEEN COMMITTEES
AND OFFICERS

It is now possible to see more clearly that other aspect of the officer's relation to the elected representative to which we referred earlier on, namely, his relation to the committee or committees with whose work he is associated, as distinct from his relation to the Council as a whole. It will have become manifest that his first contacts are in every instance with the committee. It is to the committee that he presents his reports on all matters which lie outside his own field of decision. Most matters within the Council's sphere of responsibility arise on the report made to each meeting of the committee concerned by the Head of the Department concerned, or on the correspondence submitted by the Clerk, who is the general channel of communications between the Authority and the outside world, and by whom all correspondence is conducted except such as is carried on by other Departmental Heads on matters within their executive province. In a typical report to his committee an officer will give information of work done, outline issues requiring attention or decision, and on many matters put forward suggestions or recommendations of his own. The majority of the work carried out by the officers is doubtless of a managerial, professional, or administrative type which requires no specific sanction, whether of committee or Council, so long as it is within financial allocations. There is, however, a dividing line between questions falling in this sphere and questions involving principle and policy, which is not always easily drawn; and a Departmental Head has usually many items to submit in his periodical report on which he feels it necessary to have the committee's directions. When an officer puts forward a new scheme, Standing Orders usually compel him to insert other data relevant to the topic which has been supplied by other officers; and in matters of moment his proposals will be embodied in a special report with accompanying memoranda by other officers, e.g. an engineering report will be accompanied by legal and financial memoranda.

G

In small Authorities the officers sometimes report verbally, or read their reports from a report book at the meeting. The practice in Authorities of size is for written reports to be circulated in advance, with the agenda for the meeting; and this is the only satisfactory way where business is voluminous and complex, as it is today in almost every type of Authority. Councillors should have had the opportunity of considering the relevant data before they come to discuss it at the meeting. The written report also prevents snap decisions on items brought up at the last moment; and schools the Departments into a recognition that they must continually be assembling their material in proper form for the committee's consideration. Moreover, it is of the essence of good administration to make responsibility visible; and in important matters, therefore, the data which was supplied by the officers and on which the committee has acted, or the advice the officer may have tendered, should be on record. Finally, the requirement that an officer should commit his data and proposals to paper, for individual scrutiny before the meeting, and collective discussion at it, establishes him in a habit of thinking out his proposals in clear, concrete, and definite terms. A good deal of trouble, and some expense, is involved in the issue of written reports before committees meet; but it is trouble and expense well worth while.

THE RÔLE OF COMMITTEE-CHAIRMAN

We shall not have penetrated quite to the heart of the municipal administrative system if we omit to note the functions performed by the chairmen of committees. These in practice go far beyond the functions of a chairman in controlling debate. It becomes necessary, in practice, for the close contacts established between officers and committees to be supplemented by equally close and much more frequent contacts between the officers and the chairmen of the committees. Urgent matters arise between meetings with which the officers, the only lawful agents of the Council in its dealings with the outside world, are bound to deal, and to deal promptly and decisively. In such circumstances, unless a special meeting of the committee is held, a course not always practicable, the officer must take the responsibility for the decision, and his acts will usually bind the Council. The custom in such circumstances is for the officer to consult the committee's chairman; and although the authorization to act or decide which is sometimes purported to be given by the chairman to the officer on such occasions is legally invalid (no individual member of the Council—not even a chairman—can lawfully be given power to act on its behalf) the officer does in fact often act on the chairman's advice or directions. The chairman is tacitly expected to be able to convey the sense of the committee and to know when it is safe to rely upon their subsequent confirmation, and if necessary the Council's.

The chairman of the committee is also expected to be its eyes and ears. Just as the Council looks to the committee for close knowledge of a department's work, so the committee usually looks to its chairman to be more fully acquainted with this work than the average member. Again, as a meeting is all the better conducted if the chairman knows intimately the details of the business arising beforehand, it is the custom for each Departmental Head to keep the chairman acquainted with the more important matters on which he proposes to report, and to discuss these beforehand.

The chairman also has important duties to perform in relation to the Council, and perhaps these duties are the most important of all. It is the chairman who must explain more fully the proposals, resolutions, and recommendations which the committee brings before the Council, and be the spokesman of the committee in any debates upon its work or reports. Again, it is through the opening speeches of the chairmen in submitting their committees' reports and proposals to the Council that the public is most conveniently informed of the Local Authority's work and policies.

It is obviously the chairmen of committees who are the really important element (from the administrative standpoint) among the elected personnel of our Councils. Their functions are, however, those of a rapporteur. They have no legal powers of their own; and what they achieve as individuals they must achieve, like the Mayor, chiefly through personality, and the respect which they attract. On the whole, the developing rôle of the chairmen of committees in English local government has contributed much to its efficiency in times of mounting strain and pressure; but in some places the informal and unofficial, but very real power, which chairmen may acquire has resulted in an unwholesome Caesarism. Reflection will show that the only effective safeguard against such a development is not merely the integrity, but the strength and integrity, of the chief officers, and above all of the Clerk. The officers in general, and perhaps the Clerk in particular, have a duty to the Council as a whole which transcends that of any loyalty to a chairman, or for that matter a committee, and if satisfied that either is abusing their power or trust, it is the officer's duty to bring the position to the Council's notice.

COUNCIL PROCEDURE

The system now outlined is reflected in the procedure at meetings of the Council. Most of the business there will arise on the reports and recommendations of the committees; and the volume of work so coming forward in these days is so considerable that steps have had to be taken to develop a procedure at Council meetings which will cope expeditiously with it. The system now coming into vogue is for the Clerk to call out the numbers and titles of each committee's minutes or recommendations, after these have been moved as a whole by the chairman, and seconded by the deputy chairman, of the committee concerned. On this call-over questions may be asked, and answered by the chairmen, as each number is called; but no debate takes place. If a member is opposed to any item he merely registers a formal objection to it. If there is no formal objection the item is deemed to have been passed. When the call-over is complete for all committees, and not until then, the items objected to are called on for debate. This system enables unopposed business to be cleared off quickly and debate to be concentrated on items known to be opposed. It also marks out in advance the order and scope of the controversial elements in the business. In the absence of such a system one controversial item taken in its usual order may take up the whole time of the meeting, leaving a lot of unopposed business to stand over until the next or an adjourned meeting—a course which may involve serious delay. The system is also one which, if properly regulated by an appropriate Standing Order, keeps the lines of debate very clear.

There is usually provision in Standing Orders for matters to be discussed in full Council on notice given beforehand; but so many administrative controls can be side-tracked if business takes any other course than the usual one of passage through committee, that the Standing Orders of some Councils provide that even a Notice of Motion which is carried shall stand referred to the appropriate committee for consideration and report. Practices of this kind may seem curious to the uninitiated, but there is no doubt that they prevent snap decisions taken upon inadequate information.

On the whole, it may be said that the rôle of 'full Council' in an Authority of size is becoming that of a body which registers approvals, exercises a broad control, and singles out the larger issues of policy for debate. On any balanced view this is as it should be: a Council which can debate for an hour or two some minor detail of administration, while leaving major policies unexplained and unexpounded, may be more demagogic, but not necessarily more democratic, and must obviously lack an administrative sense. The real workshops of local government are the committees. It is regrettable that this feature, imperative and salutary as it may be on administrative grounds, sometimes deprives the full meetings of the Council of much that is of interest from the standpoint of the outside beholder. A little more conscious effort on the part of the chairmen in presenting their committees' reports could, however, do much to remedy this state of affairs.

The proceedings in Council are more formal than in committee and are usually controlled by rules of debate forming part of Standing Orders. Rules of this kind are obviously more needful when the assembly is larger. Except in business required to be transacted at an Annual Meeting, no business can be transacted at a meeting of a Borough or County Council unless it is specified in the summons sent out at least three clear days beforehand. It is sometimes forgotten that this rule is statutory and mandatory, and cannot be waived by the Council's consent. Curiously enough, the rule is not applicable to District Councils. Whether it is applied to the business of committees depends upon the Standing Orders of the Councils concerned.

The facilities which Local Authorities must afford to the Press are prescribed by the Local Authorities (Admission of the Press to Meetings) Act 1908 and the Public Bodies (Admission of the Press) Act 1960, and include access to meetings of the

Council and its Committees, subject to temporary exclusions under specific resolution passed by the Council on the ground of public interest. The latter Act requires facilities to be given for the attendance of members of the public.

There are occasions when the full Council itself sits as a committee, e.g. when the issues of policy are so large that they should be considered in detail as well as in private by the full Council-in-Committee before they are officially formulated for recommendation to full 'open council'. When sitting as a Council-in-Committee or Committee of the Whole, the decisions are subject to confirmation at a formal session of the Council. But this position does not affect the right of an Authority by resolution under the Act of 1908 to exclude the Press even at a formal meeting and take a valid and final decision in their absence. A meeting of the Council-in-Committee summoned as such can, however, only have status as a committee; and even when, during a formal meeting, a resolution is carried to 'go into Committee', and the Press are excluded, the Council often resumes Open Council to take and record its decision on the subject-matter discussed 'in Committee'.

Committees submit their proceedings or recommendations to the Council in the form of minutes or reports, printed and circulated beforehand with or soon after the summons and agenda. We need not enter here into the very technical question of whether minutes or reports are preferable. Whichever be adopted, it is manifest that the form in which committees report to Council must fulfil several aims. The minutes or reports must so embody the committee's activities or recommendation as to make sure that the Council understands clearly what it is being told or advised. They must also constitute carefully worded instruction for the departments and officers concerned; and finally, and as far as legal limitations and administrative requirements permit, they should embody such information as will enable the public, when the proceedings are reported by the Press, to understand broadly the issue discussed. These three considerations are not easy to reconcile. They tax the judgment and drafting skill of Clerks not a little, particularly when the issues are affected by the law of libel, from which Local Authorities are not immune.

STANDING ORDERS

The foregoing account of the administrative process has been but a sketch of its elementary features. The relations of Council's committees, departments, and officers all require the closest adjustment if satisfactory control, co-ordination, and efficient executive work are to be achieved. For this very reason it is essential that the system which the individual Authority evolves in the light of local conditions and experience should be embodied in such a way that everyone may know it, or be able to find out easily what it is, and what should be done to conform with it in daily practice. Such an embodiment is most appropriately and conveniently made in Standing Orders. It is a great mistake to conceive of these as only concerned with rules of debate at meetings of Council. They should be a complete articulation of the Council's administrative arrangements, a continuous embodiment of all administrative rules which evolve in practice or are laid down by resolution from time to time. It is useless for resolutions dealing with administrative methods and requirements to be left embedded in old minutes, or other scattered sources, not easily accessible to departmental heads and their key subordinates. A full and detailed, even an elaborate, set of Standing Orders is not, as the ignorant think, a mark of 'the official mind', but the expression of a well-thought-out and well-tried system of administration, running smoothly in the light of day.

But the system, however elaborate, should never be regarded as static. Each year brings substantial change in one local government service or another, and such changes are bound to have repercussions upon administrative mechanism, and in particular upon the organization of committee work and upon departmental structure. The system should be periodically reviewed; and since it is, or ought to be, embodied in Standing Orders, the best way of securing such a review is to provide for an annual revision of Standing Orders, and in particular an annual review of the lay-out of Standing Committees and the distribution of powers among them. This in practice is what the most efficient Local Authorities do. In some places the Standing Orders are revised, after report and recommendations from the Clerk, by the Selection Committee which meets after the elections to make recommendations to the ensuing Annual Meeting as to the constitution and personnel of committees. In others the job is done by the General Purposes Committee.

COMPARISONS

The municipal system of administration has virtues which rest upon the fact that the administration is local—conducted by a local agency, for a local body of consumers or citizens, and under local supervision and control—but it is the committee system which makes these virtues more fully and easily attainable. In probably no other sphere of administration is it possible for the official machine to be so amenable to the control of the elected representatives, or for the expert and the amateur to collaborate in the formulation of policy in the ways we have referred to. It is not only, however, the relationship between elected personnel and officials to which the virtues of the municipal system are traceable. The system renders possible a close and beneficial contact between the municipal machine and the consumers and citizens it serves. The Standing Committee is a body noticeably accessible to the citizens served, and it collects their complaints, criticisms, and suggestions over wide angles. The committee-room is a focal point at which these can be submitted and examined across the table with those responsible for the conduct of the service.

Conditions in the Parliamentary sphere are markedly different. In theory, the Executive is accountable to Parliament, but Parliament does not organize itself into Standing Committees except for the purpose of considering draft legislation, and the Members of Parliament cannot possibly get to know the civil servants and their work in the way that local Councils and committees know the municipal departments. In fact, the work of Government Departments is so immense, their activities so widespread, and the link between them and the elective assembly so slight, that the average Member of Parliament can hardly see their work, still less know or judge it. There is, of course, the safeguard of the Parliamentary Question. This cannot be a substitute for the close and continuous vigilance exercised by the Standing Committee of a municipality. It fosters care, and sometimes undue caution, rather than stimulates zeal. On the occasions. and in the atmosphere in which it is asked, it operates as a sanction. The Civil Servant has no such opportunity as the municipal servant has, to discuss his actions with the elected representatives in an atmosphere of friendly collaboration, or to test in privacy their reactions to his advice.

Those public services which are run by 'Public Corporations' or qualified Boards, with little or no supervision by elected representatives at all, are largely free even from the safeguard of the Parliamentary Question. The machinery necessary for their management is not, in all of them, of the kind which can also articulate the consumers' views and interests and bring them to bear upon management in the ways so easily and naturally available in the sphere of local government. It is not our business here to discuss what measures are or might be taken in these other spheres of public service to promote a responsiveness to public control which comes about so easily and naturally in the municipal sphere; but it would be doing less than justice to municipal administration not to notice its characteristic virtues. Of course, every system has its defects; and the defects of the municipal system, and of the committee system in particular are, in the main, the defects of its virtues. These we discuss in Chapter X.

CHAPTER VII

Committee Organization

KINDS OF COMMITTEE

BEFORE WE DISCUSS the principles of committee lay-out and other aspects of committee organization let us see what different kinds of committees there are.

The first distinction is between statutory and permissive committees. The former are those which the Local Authority is compelled by statute to set up, and the latter those which it sets up at its own discretion under the general enabling power now contained in the Local Government Act of 1933. Statutory committees usually owe their existence to Acts which established new services for which the legislature deemed administration through committees indispensable, and sometimes felt it necessary to prescribe the kind of committee to be set up. The prescriptions vary. In some instances the Local Authority is merely directed to work the service through a committee, and this can be an existing or a new one. In others, the Local Authority is directed to establish a committee for that particular service alone. In such latter instances, the Local Authority has sometimes been given directions as to the composition of the committee. Thus, the provisions requiring the establishment of Education, Maternity and Child Welfare, and Housing Committees, have provided for the co-option of representatives of particular 'interests', or persons with special knowledge or experience, or for the inclusion of a minimum number of women. It would be fruitless in a work of this description to list the statutory committees—since they vary with the particular types of Authority—or to detail the prescriptions applicable to them. It was acknowledged in the last chapter that the field covered by statutory committees is not a large one compared with the field which the Local Authority covers under permissive powers and in which it is free to set up the kind of committee organization which it finds best suited to its particular range of work. It may nevertheless be said here that it

COMMITTEE ORGANIZATION 107

would be better if all prescriptions for statutory committees were abolished or consolidated into a simple prescription for a given number of co-opted members whose choice could be provided for by Ministerial Order. Parliamentary prescription tends to be static and rapidly becomes anomalous in consequence. When a new service is established it may often be wise to take special precautions that people with some interest in it should participate in its administration, but specific directions to this end lose their relevance after a time and become antiquated. The need to meet such direction often prevents a revision of committee lay-out to meet changed conditions over the whole sphere of the Local Authority's work.

The next distinction to be noted is between Standing and Special Committees. Standing Committees are those which the Local Authority either appoints indefinitely, or continues in practice to appoint at each Annual Meeting to hold office throughout the currency of the municipal administrative year. The Standing Committees are usually those to which business arising under the Council's continuing functions is distributed, e.g. the management of a particular service or the discharge of a continuing function, such as financial control. Those of the Standing Committees which manage services with the funds voted by the Council are often referred to as Service Committees; and those which in so doing control a particular Department are often called Departmental Committees as distinct from those incidentally served by a Department or Departments. Special Committees are those appointed to deal with a specific question or with a passing need which does not conveniently fall within the province of a Standing Committee— e.g. to investigate a new problem, a proposed new service, or some special administrative issue.

Some Special Committees, however, are regularly appointed from time to time for recurring purposes. Such, for example, is the Selection Committee, appointed to recommend the personnel for Standing Committees, and often invested with the duty of revising Standing Orders and the terms of reference to Standing Committees. Another example is the committee appointed by some Local Authorities to consider the choice of Mayor. There is a universal feeling that as this process necessarily involves the discussion of personalities, it is best to arrive at a choice by a process of internal discussion and understand-

ing, through the medium of a committee making recommendations to an informal meeting of the Council, rather than to
debate a choice in open Council. Sometimes the choice of
Mayor rotates by party choice from year to year, according to
the balance of strength of the parties on the Council; but even
where this custom prevails a Mayoralty Committee is usually
appointed. Even party understandings should be subject to
some safeguards for the good character and acceptable personality of the person on whom the party choice falls. In any
event, the Council has to fix a salary for the Mayor; and this is
better arrived at on the recommendation of a Mayoralty Committee, after consideration of the local conditions in the particular year for which the choice is being made, and after
contact with the nominee to be put forward for the office.

ALTERNATIVE PRINCIPLES FOR
FORMING COMMITTEES

There are two conceivable methods of allocating business to
Standing Committees; according to the varying objects of the
Council's activity, or according to the kinds of work its activity
involves. The first method resolves itself, in practice, into a
distribution of work according to services, such as Health,
Education, or Water Supply, and the establishment of a Standing Committee for each service or for particular groups of
services. The second method would involve the establishment
of a committee to deal with legal and secretarial work, a committee to deal with finance, a committee to deal with
medical work, a committee to deal with engineering work, and
so on.

It is the former method which first established itself in
English local government, and which still predominates in it.
With the exception of the direction to County Councils and
Metropolitan Boroughs to set up a Finance Committee, all
statutory directions to set up committees are directions to set
up committees for a given object or service. It may indeed be
doubted whether a complete organization of committee work
on the opposite principle would be feasible: concern with
means would prevent any sight of the end. So far as is known, a
complete articulation of committee work on this second principle has never been tried. Committees so established are, how-

ever, a useful, and in fact an indispensable adjunct, to a lay-out based on the usual principle. A Finance Committee, a Staff Committee, and a Works Committee are committees organized according to the work to be done, and the two first at any rate, are common form in English local government today, for reasons which we mention later.

There are three considerations which the author considers it is imperative to observe in determining the committees to be established by any Local Authority, and the division of business among them.

First, the whole business of the Council, actual or possible, should be so distributed as never to leave the location of any particular subject in doubt. This rule is dictated by the proposition put forward in the last chapter: that the administrative process is so centred around committees that business cannot flow through any other channels without considerable risk that decisions will be taken with inadequate consideration, or upon insufficient or inaccurate data. The only way to ensure a complete and unambiguous distribution of business is to formulate a detailed list of the duties of each committee, embodied either in its terms of reference when it is appointed at the Annual Meeting, or in Standing Orders; and, in either event, to keep this list up to date by some such system of annual revision as we referred to in the last chapter. Nevertheless, when the most careful thought has been given to a list of duties, items inevitably arise which may not be covered in the terms of reference to any existing committee. To guard against this contingency the Council should either designate a separate committee to take charge of any residue of unspecified business, or assign such residue to an existing committee. The appointment of a General Purposes Committee comprising all members of the Council, to exercise a roving commission, involving conflict with Standing Committees, or to rehash business brought before other committees, or to act as a permanent Council-in-Committee to deal regularly with awkward matters in the absence of the Press so as to evade the Act of 1908, are practices which cannot be too strongly condemned. But the establishment of a General Purposes Committee for handling any unallocated residue of business is a piece of administrative wisdom. There is much to be said for the practice of making the Finance Committee also a General Purposes Committee, since there is usually a financial angle to matters which arise unexpectedly.

The second consideration to be observed in committee layout is this: that the grouping of duties under separate committees should follow well-recognized branches of the Local Authority's activity, and not be left to follow the whim of the members of the Local Authority at a particular time. There are certain important services which obviously call for separate committees to deal with each of them, e.g. Education, Housing, Public Health, or Sanitation. There are smaller services which can hardly justify a separate committee. It is in respect of these that the second principle put forward is most important; for it means that the primary aim should be the best possible combination of these smaller fields of activity in the light of administrative requirements generally and the necessity for co-ordination in particular. There are, no doubt, some respects in which the municipal machine must adjust itself to the man; but administrative efficiency can be so upset by bad committee organization that committee organization is a sphere in which the man should adjust himself to the machine. The destination of some kinds of municipal business is, however, not always obvious, even on administrative considerations. There is an enormous variety of regulative work which is difficult of classification, and which may have no obvious affiliations with the work of committees operating single large services, or well-marked groups. What is to be done with functions such as these? The author suggests that it is usually better to graft these miscellaneous items on to the terms of refence of some of the major committees rather than to establish separate committees; but this view is really dependent on the third principle we put forward as a guide to the lay-out of committees.

This may briefly be stated as 'the fewer the committees the better'. Thus baldly stated, the principle is open to challenge. It would obviously be impossible so to concentrate the business among a few committees as to call upon these committees for sessions of six or seven hours in the evenings. Human considerations must be taken into account. Nevertheless, the maxim has much virtue as a corrective. There is a tendency in many Councils, particularly those which pride themselves upon their democratic temper, to believe that work will be better done if there are many committees. Such a belief often depends upon an exaggerated view of the importance attaching to special experience or knowledge of a particular subject on the part of the lay personnel. It may also be due to a feeling that to establish a separate committee for every question or duty which may assume a temporary importance or urgency shows zeal and determination, and can produce better results. Besides precluding the maximum possibility of co-ordination, the establishment of more committees than is strictly necessary is bad on psychological grounds. It is a well-observed fact that every committee tends to develop a corporate spirit of its own. This in itself may be good, but its polar aspect is a misplaced sense of independence which easily generates friction with other committees. If each committee is dealing with fundamentally different kinds of work no great harm need be done. If committees proliferate, in spheres which are not dissimilar, a great deal of harm can be done. Municipal administration and municipal committees are not alone in such potentialities as these. It has been noticed by many students of constitutional and administrative machinery, that if two bodies are established to work side by side, even without any fundamental cleavage of interest, they inevitably generate a certain amount of friction. It is for these reasons that it is best to observe in administration the maxim which the medieval logicians laid down for the process of logical division: *Entia non sunt praeter necessitatem multiplicanda*: 'Entities should not be gratuitiously multiplied.'

COMPOSITION OF COMMITTEES

The size of committees is largely at the option of the Local Authority. There is a fairly wide recognition that a smaller committee works best, but this consideration has sometimes to be tempered by the feeling, in authorities such as County Councils, that there should be a fair balance of representation from the various parts of the area. In the more compact urban areas there is hardly the same need. In some of the smaller and older Boroughs the feeling that committees should be constituted of a member from each Ward still lingers, but it is seldom that this principle is observed in towns of larger size.

Before 1933 most of the statutory committees had to include a quota of co-opted members, chosen from the sources and in the ways laid down by the relevant Statute; but there was no general power of co-optation. Since 1933 there has been a general provision enabling Local Authorities to co-opt non-members of the Council to all committees of the Council except the Finance Committee, persons so appointed usually being called co-opted members. At least two-thirds of the members of every committee must, however, be members of the Local Authority, thus ensuring a substantial margin for Council control, even if the committee be given delegated powers. This general power does not disturb any special arrangements to be observed in relation to the *statutory* committees. The new enabling powers of the Act of 1933 have not been extensively used; and there seems little doubt that the practice of co-optation does not find favour with the Local Authorities. The intention was obviously to enable persons who have special knowledge or experience, and who may have neither the time nor inclination for the full responsibilities of a councillor, to give their services in a limited field. The feeling of the average councillor is that members of the Council are not expected to have special capacities; that it would be best if committees did not pretend to be any more than they were, namely, bodies of laymen exercising the functions expected of lay-men, and which it is of special value for lay-men to perform; and that in these days special knowledge and experience are best looked for in the proper quarter, i.e. among the officers. There is also a feeling that those exercising public responsibilities should always pass through the gateway of popular election.

In this connection the composition of committees responsible for the Police is worthy of special mention. Police authorities are (subject to a few exceptions) the county councils and county boroughs. Before the Police Act, 1964, borough police were supervised by the Watch Committee of the Council, but in the counties this duty was performed by a Joint Standing Committee composed of equal numbers of county J.P.s, nominated by Quarter Sessions, and of members of the county council. This arrangement was unsatisfactory because the Joint Standing Committee was an independent body with a right to impose a precept on the county rate; since half its members had no responsibility to the electorate, the principle of no taxation without representation was in jeopardy. The 1964 Police Act has altered this situation in replacing the independent Standing Joint Committees by Police Committees of the county councils of whose members one-third are J.P.s nominated by Quarter Sessions. Similarly, one-third of the Watch Committees in boroughs now consist of borough justices nominated by the local bench. There was some objection to the introduction of a non-elected element into Watch Committees, but the Government view was that the experience of magistrates would be valuable on matters of borough police administration.

We have already noticed a not uncommon rule that a Mayor shall not be chairman of a Standing Committee during his year of office, and the reasons which have led to such a prohibition. The Mayor is usually allowed, however, to continue his membership of committees, and appointed personally to the committees on which he would have served had he not been Mayor. In addition, many Authorities provide that he shall be an *ex officio* member of every Standing Committee, along with any Deputy he may appoint. This does not mean that the Mayor is expected to enlarge his committee work during his year of office. In fact, as we have already said, the contrary is the case. The object of the arrangement is to give him access to the committees for discussion, information, and exchanges of view which may assist him in the discharge of Mayoral duties. Whether the Mayor and Deputy Mayor are to have a vote as *ex officio* members is dependent upon the Council's express wishes, and the practice varies.

There are many towns in which the Chairman of the Finance Committee is also made an *ex officio* member of each Standing Committee, so that he may follow the course of the more important schemes emanating from the Standing Committees from their very inception, or hold a watching brief at critical times. It is not suggested that this is an essential step in financial control, particularly when appropriate Standing Orders on this subject are in force on lines later to be mentioned, or when the Borough Treasurer or his representative is in regular attendance at Standing Committees, as is almost universally the case. But the practice is a useful supplement.

DELEGATION OF POWERS TO COMMITTEES

A Council may use its committees in two ways. It may either

H

direct that business in the allotted sphere shall first be considered by the committee, which shall then make recommendations thereon to the Council on which the Council will decide; or it may authorize the committee to decide certain matters as though it were the Council, either reporting its decisions or not, as the Council directs. In this latter case the Council is said to be delegating its powers.

Before 1933 a Council's ability to delegate to its committees was limited, or confined to specified spheres; but the Act of 1933 gave Local Authorities permission to delegate any or all of their powers and duties to committees, with only two reservations, namely, the power to borrow money and the power to levy a rate. The permission could hardly be more generous. It secures the Council's control over the purse-strings, both in regard to revenue to be raised and capital to be expended, control over capital expenditure also carrying with it the scrutiny of the schemes to be capitalized; otherwise it enables the committees to look after everything else without prior recourse to the Council. That the legislature should have seen fit to confer so wide a permission as this reflects the enormous volume of work which Local Authorities must handle. Generous as the enabling powers are, the larger Authorities could hardly do with anything less. It is believed that in the largest cities the measure of delegation goes almost to the statutory limit, and the same may be true of most of the County Councils. In the Counties, meetings of the full Council cannot be frequent; and it is easy to see that the measure of delegation must be full if public business is not to be intolerably delayed through the need for the decisions of committees to await the confirmation of the Council.

It is well to remember, however, that delegation is not without its disadvantages. It induces a less watchful habit on the part of the Council as a whole, and it usually means that the average member of the Council is only in touch with a fraction of its total activity. He is a member of one or two committees; and learns little of the work of other committees and takes but a nominal responsibility for it. This need not be the case, since it is possible for the full Council to be informed of the activities of a committee which discharges even the fullest range of delegated powers. In practice, reports after the event are seldom full. Indeed, much of the virtue of delegation would be lost if a committee exercising delegated powers had to report its decisions on every item. It remains true that, where substantial delegation exists, as for example in the County Councils, much of the Council's administration goes on unseen and unknown by the members as a whole. For this reason critics of the County Council system of government argue that the inevitably large measure of delegation which it involves is one of its strongest drawbacks.

Be that is it may, the measure of delegated power to be given by any particular authority to its committees calls fairly obviously for a careful balancing of advantage and disadvantage. In areas of moderate size, and in the compact town areas, even the larger ones, where the Council can meet fairly frequently, and where it often meets in the evening hours to suit the members' convenience, delegation need seldom go to its full permitted limits. For example, where the Council is meeting monthly, with a regular monthly cycle of committee meetings, and where special meetings can be fairly easily arranged to deal with urgent matters of importance, there is not much point in delegating powers over a wide field: the acts of the committees can in any event come before the Council and be settled in a week or two. In many of the more moderately sized towns, delegation is confined either to matters of pure routine, or to matters which have to be decided within narrow limits of time under legal requirements. It is particularly important that a Committee's delegated powers should be closely defined, and distinguished in its list of duties from its functions of consideration and recommendation. Here also is an aspect of the Authority's administration which should be subject to annual revision.

THE PLACE OF SUB-COMMITTEES

It is a fairly common practice for Standing Committees to appoint either standing or special sub-committees from time to time. If it is intended that a sub-committee should exercise delegated powers they should be conferred on the sub-committee by the Council so as to obviate any invalidity arising from the legal rule—*delegatus non potest delegare*. There should be some watchfulness over the practice of appointing sub-committees. Some Committees tend to appoint a sub-committee to consider every little difficulty that may crop up in the main committee. At the other extreme, some committees will insist on handling a lot of routine business which might well be left to a sub-committee which comprises members with more time or interest in that routine than their colleagues. It is usually for routine business that sub-committees are most useful, and for routine business it is better for the committee to appoint a standing sub-committee for the year. This course is often best from every standpoint. There may occasionally be need for a sub-committee with some special experience or special interests to consider business of greater import—in which event a special sub-committee may be justified. The special issues which a main committee finds it useful to refer first to a sub-committee are usually, however, such as call for the expenditure of a little time in patient sifting of the issues rather than for special knowledge; and they can usually be dealt with more regularly and promptly, and with less likelihood of being side-tracked, by a standing sub-committee. Large schemes and important issues of policy are better discussed by the main committee.

THE FINANCE COMMITTEE AND ITS WORK

In the remaining part of this chapter we shall consider the work of committees established on the second of the principles to which we referred in the opening part of this chapter, namely, the nature of the work to be done; and first we shall notice the work of the Finance Committee, and the associated procedure which establishes the Council's financial control over the work of its committees, and, indeed, over the whole of the administrative process.

It is humorously said that the English can do nothing without appointing a committee. So true is this in local government that Local Authorities appoint a committee even to overcome the defects of the committee system itself. In theory the Council is responsible for taking a conspectus of the whole of its work, and of the activities of its committees, for balancing the needs of one committee or service with another, for deciding the amount of money to be expended over the whole field each year, for making the necessary allocations, and for seeing that the financial arrangements so settled for the year are duly observed—in a word, for passing the budget and for seeing that the budgetary provision is not exceeded without the Council's knowledge. In practice a large body such as a full Council, obsessed with important and often controversial issues of principle and policy, can rarely form such a conspectus, or co-ordinate its agents to the ends above mentioned, unless it specially equips itself to do so. The instrument with which the Council equips itself to exercise these functions is its Finance Committee, which is usually also charged with a general supervision of the Council's accounting arrangements, the payment of its accounts, and the collection of its revenues.

There are only two types of Authority in which a Finance Committee must be appointed by Statute, i.e. County Councils and Metropolitan Boroughs. Excepting areas in which the Council is so small, and its functions so narrow, as to involve it in no difficulties of oversight and co-ordination, it is nevertheless almost a universal practice for English Local Authorities to appoint a Finance Committee.

There is still much controversy as to the type of committee which is best suited to the work, since this involves a watchfulness over other committees, and over all the departments, and the prior consideration of circumstances giving rise to overspendings and supplementary estimates. One method of selection is to appoint chairmen of the Standing Committees to the Finance Committee; this enables the chairmen to explain and defend the viewpoint of their committees when asking the Finance Committee for authority to spend money. It can be argued that if some chairmen are on the Finance Committee, then all should be to prevent some committees obtaining unfair advantage. Another method of selection is to appoint members chosen for their special interest and ability in financial matters and to avoid selecting committee chairmen. Such a committee may well be able to take a more detached and independent view of various proposals for expenditure, whereas a Finance Committee composed of committee chairmen may tend to bargain and compromise in a spending direction rather than a saving direction. A third method is to combine these two techniques, to have committee chairmen together with additional members to provide a neutral element; this system may be the best unless it produces a committee of inordinate size. Where a council is run on strictly party lines, a Finance Committee of chairmen would, of course, produce a one-party committee which is clearly unsatisfactory.

Budgetary Procedure.—The medium through which the Council, with the help of its Finance Committee, finances the services, and controls the expenditure upon them, is the Annual Budget. There is no document which can be called by this name, and the term is used in the same broad sense in which it is used in the Parliamentary sphere, to denote a three-fold process, namely:—the formulation of annual estimates of income and expenditure as the basis for deciding what taxation (i.e. rate) to levy; the levy of the rate; and the allocation of the rate-revenue to the various heads of expenditure. In local government, however, the third process does not, as in the Parliamentary sphere, result in a constitutionally separate process of appropriations to the heads of expenditure. The estimates as finally settled when the rate is decided constitute the appropriations which the several Standing Committees are to observe. It follows that the estimates should be prepared under suitable and effective heads and sub-headings. The budgetary process does not constitute full 'financial control' as now exercised by progressive Authorities. It is the necessary minimum, and is a process imposed by statute; the preparation of estimates being compulsory, and the statutes directing the rate to be levied with due regard to the Estimates.

The Local Authorities' financial year begins on 1st April and, as we can appreciate, the budgetary process must start considerably beforehand. It starts, at departmental level, by the preparation of draft estimates by the executive head of each department. The fact that, at a later stage, the Borough Treasurer as an officer of the Finance Committee will be expected to express to the Finance Committee his independent views upon the estimates need not preclude close contact between him and the executive head at the stage of departmental drafting—particularly on questions of fact and calculation. The estimates prepared by the departmental head are then circulated to the Standing Committee concerned, and scrutinized item by item. It is then for the Standing Committee to adopt them, or to revise or amend them, and to put them forward to the Finance Committee. The Finance Committee then meet, usually at a special meeting, to go through all the Standing Committees' estimates. At this stage they have before them, or ought to have before them, the report of the Borough Treasurer upon the estimates as such, upon the level of rateable value which can be expected for the ensuing financial year, and upon all other relevant facts which will enable the Finance Committee to form a conspectus of the Committees' requirements or proposals and of the Local Authority's related financial position. The Finance Committee must then make up its mind whether the estimates of the Standing Committees are to stand, or, if not, what amendments are to be made; and must at some stage put forward its recommendations to the Council as to the rate to be levied to cover the decisions it takes upon the estimates.

It is possible for the procedure at this stage to vary, and it does in fact vary as between one Local Authority and another. In some places, before reporting to the Council its own recommendations, the Finance Committee refers the estimates back to the Standing Committees if it does not approve them, and indicates the amendments it considers necessary. In other places the chairman of the Standing Committees attend before the Finance Committee, and by common understanding are regarded as empowered to make concessions to the Finance Committee on behalf of their Committees. Again, in some places the estimates are put forward as originally submitted by the Standing Committees, with separate indications of the Finance Committee's proposals for revision; while in other places the estimates circulated to the Council only show the estimates as they were amended and passed by the Finance Committee.

Consistently with the wide degree of freedom given to Local Authorities over their rate-borne expenditure, the statutory prescriptions as to the considerations to be observed in making a rate are framed in broad terms. It is nevertheless important to notice that some such prescriptions exist. The rate must cover the estimated expenditure for the period, the requirements of any Authorities which precept upon the Rating Authority, and any existing deficiencies in the rate fund. No provision can lawfully be made in the estimates for a general reserve fund, but there is a direction to include in the estimates such additional amounts as in the opinion of the Authority are requisite (1) to meet contingencies during the period of the rate, and (2) to defray expenditure which has to be met before the revenue from the next rate is received. This latter amount, called 'the working balance', is usually used to adjust slight fluctuations which might ensue if a rate were levied on the exact amount of the Estimate, but it is not proper to appropriate any substantial sum from this balance in aid of rate. A working balance is available, however, for contingencies, and, if maintained at a satisfactory level, may obviate the inclusion of any large specific sum for contingencies.

Decisions on the Annual Budget are usually taken by the Council at its March meeting. No special procedure is necessary at the Council for the fixing of the rate. The rate is 'made' in the legal sense by the Council's resolution; so that second thoughts are not possible at an ensuing meeting of the Council, though it is competent for the Local Authority subsequently to make a Supplementary Rate, even during the currency of a rate already made. The procedure for the making of the rate was formerly complicated by the association of rating procedure with the Guardians and the Justices; but this antiquated procedure has now been swept away, and all that need now be done is for the rate to be published, as required by statute, when the Council have made it.

Financial Control.—The Annual Budget, on the lines prescribed by statute, is itself a medium of financial control. The growing complexity and volume of business render it the bare minimum; and most Local Authorities have found it necessary or desirable to proceed to further measures, to ensure a closer correlation of expenditure to the Local Authority's financial position, and a close observance of budgetary allocations. In fact, it is these further measures that are usually spoken of in local government circles as 'financial control' rather than the budgetary process itself. They are usually implemented, and ought to be implemented, if they are to be really effective, in a carefully drawn set of financial Standing Orders.

Financial Standing Orders are of necessity complex, and it would be out of place to describe them in detail here. Their broad objects are, however, capable of very brief and simple statement. The primary object is to ensure that the budgetary allocations are not exceeded; as in a large organism they can very easily be, unless the progress of work and expenditure could be kept under hourly watch throughout the financial year. There can, of course, be no absolute guarantee against excess expenditure. The objects of the financial Standing Orders are to fix responsibility for any such excess, and to enable it to be detected before it goes far—in a word, to prevent over-expenditure in the same way as the police prevent crime. Responsibility is therefore placed upon departmental heads, in submitting any proposals for carrying out works or making a purchase, to state whether the cost is or is not covered by estimates. Some Authorities go further and require proposals which were not contemplated when the estimates were framed to be specially indicated even though they may be a general head of expenditure in the estimates which would cover them. Committees too are placed under a duty of not knowingly incurring expenditure in excess of estimates unless they receive the Finance Committee's approval to a Supplementary Estimate. The Borough Treasurer is directed to submit periodical reports of the progress of expenditure in relation to estimates, and in relation to the expenditure of the preceding year. To render these controls effective it is also necessary to ensure that anything caught by the financial Standing Orders is immediately brought up to the Finance Committee. The Finance Committee is thus enabled to maintain a continuous supervision and to report to the Council from time to time.

If properly worked out, the system can be most effective. There can be little excuse for any substantial over-spending, and in practice little margin left for it. In some Authorities, indeed, the system tends to be carried to excess, and the procedure in procuring sanction for small and excusably unforeseen items of expenditure is rendered too cumbrous. Nevertheless the system, even if rigid, is a salutary one, similar in its essentials to that maintained by large business enterprises, and often going far beyond the measure of control exercised in the average business firm.

We have so far been dealing with revenue expenditure, and it remains to say that financial Standing Orders also apply controls over capital expenditure. All schemes involving loans have usually to be referred to the Finance Committee so that they may advise the Council on the financial aspects of the scheme in relation to the Local Authority's commitments generally. Some Local Authorities provide that large schemes should stand over for consideration until the next Council meeting after the meeting at which the proposals have been submitted by the Standing Committee concerned. It is also usual to make expenditure out of Reserve or Renewal Funds subject to Finance Committee approval.

THE STAFF COMMITTEE

The Staff Committee is a permissive committee and is a fairly recent innovation in committee lay-out. The Hadow Departmental Committee on the Recruitment, Training, and Qualification of Local Government Officers which reported in 1934 recommended the setting up of such committees by Authorities generally, and the response by the Local Authorities has been considerable. Even before 1934, however, the larger Authorities were beginning to introduce such committees, for reasons not dissimilar from those which called at an earlier stage of development for the appointment of Finance Committees.

The growing diversity of the Local Authorities' functions has required the assembly of staff of very different kinds, over which it is not easy for the full Council to maintain an adequate and detailed oversight. For psychological reasons, scrupulous consistency is required in the management of staff, and in the settlement of grading in the several branches of the Authority's work; and this consideration alone points to the importance of the continuous attention and scrutiny which can be given by a separate committee. Again, even before the growth of collective bargaining machinery for the Local Government Service at large, as described in the next chapter, the larger Authorities were introducing grading schemes, and it was difficult for a number of Standing Committees, each controlling a particular service, to apply schemes of this kind without serious risk of anomaly and inconsistency as between one Department and another. Even today when the broad framework of service conditions is settled on a basis of national uniformities by Whitley machinery, the volume of work which still falls to the individual Local Authority in staffing and staff management is considerable and the need for consistency as great if not greater than ever.

Nevertheless, the establishment of a Staff Committee has not everywhere meant that questions relating to staff pay, conditions, recruitment, and qualifications are concentrated in its hands. Some Councils take the view that such a concentration is neither necessary nor desirable. Long before Staff Committees were established, those Standing Committees which controlled particular services were also 'employing Committees' in the sense that they engaged and managed the official staff of the department conducting the service, even though a standard scheme was in existence, applicable to the Corporation staff as a whole. It has been argued that these committees, whose function it is to conduct the service, and who must do this through the employees engaged in it, can form a much closer and more intimate knowledge of those employees than a Staff Committee with no service responsibilities. Accordingly, in some places the Staff Committee is left to deal with the application of general schemes of pay, conditions, and grading, etc., to give its approval to the establishment of each department, as recommended by the Standing Committee, and to consider the proposals of the Standing Committees for re-gradings and new posts; while the Standing Committee is left to make appointments, and to recommend promotions and re-gradings subject to Staff Committee scrutiny.

Without going into detail, it may be said that where functions are divided in this way, the result seldom proves satisfactory. It is difficult to make any enduring demarcation of functions, for conditions relating to staff are continually changing; and even if the demarcation could be perfect or static, the passage of views and details from one Committee to another can be a very slow, cumbrous, and irritating process. There is probably one function which is best left to the Standing Committee, namely the appointment, on terms settled by the Staff Committee, of officers who wholly or primarily serve that Standing Committee. Apart from this, there is overwhelming administrative advantage in concentrating all functions relating to staff pay, allowances, conditions of service, recruitment, training, and qualifications in the hands of the Staff Committee. Even more so than in the case of the Finance Committee, it is desirable that the Staff Committee should include the chairmen of Standing Committees. From what was said in the last chapter, they must obviously acquire an intimate knowledge of the departmental staffs. A small neutral element is valuable here, however, as it is on the Finance Committee, if the total number is not thereby made too high.

THE WORKS COMMITTEE

The setting up of a Works Committee is a rather more controversial subject. Ordinarily, the department carrying out works, by direct labour or contract, and whether it be a special Works Department, or a major department of the Local Authority such as the Borough Engineer's Department, administering services which directly serve the public and not acting merely in a ministerial capacity to other departments, discharges its responsibilities under the instructions of the particular Standing Committee governing the service concerned. Thus the Borough Engineer will take his instructions from the Health Committee, if that deals with sewage, and the Highways Committee, if that deals with roads, and so on; and the Standing Committees may be expected to maintain a lively interest in work which serves their own administrative ends. It is doubtful, therefore, whether anyone can say that a Works Committee is an indispensable need.

It is argued, however, that the carrying out of works, and particularly the letting of contracts, and the consideration of the somewhat difficult issues which arise in the execution of contracts from time to time, are better handled by one committee which can correlate experience in several fields and bring a riper and fuller experience to bear upon such issues. It is argued, moreover, that it will be all to the good if the committees governing the services are relieved of the trouble and difficulty of supervising the works they have to put in hand from time to time, for these are but means towards the ends which are their primary concern, i.e. the services as given to the public; and that it is to the advantage and help of the Standing Committees if they are left free to concentrate on these ends.

The issue is not an easy one for discussion here, but it was felt worth while mentioning as an example of the tendency for committee structure to become more complex as the Local Authority's work grows in size and complexity. That projects of this kind should so continuously come under discussion in Local Government is a sign of its responsiveness to change and growth.

CHAPTER VIII

Departmental Organization

AN ACCOUNT OF the organization and nature of each municipal department would take us far beyond the scope and objects of a work such as this. We may, however, usefully indicate the salient features of departmental structure and the mechanisms which bring the departments into action—individually or in combination. To this end it is first necessary to acquaint the reader with the characteristics of the Local Government Service as a whole.

THE LOCAL GOVERNMENT SERVICE

The officers of English Local Authorities do not constitute a single body such as the Civil Service, employed by one master. Each authority determines its own establishment of staff and appoints its own officers. Except in those instances (already noticed) in which appointments or dismissal is subject to Ministerial consent, and in the few cases in which there is some central prescription of qualifications, e.g. Medical Officers and Public Health Inspectors, each Authority is free to recruit its officers in its own way, and to impose what qualifications it desires. Nevertheless, the whole body of Local Government Officers possesses many uniform characteristics and has in recent years conformed in increasing measure to standards and uniformities introduced into pay, service conditions, entry and promotion tests, and many other elements in the officer's contract of service with his employing authority.

These developments are due, partly to Trade Union organization among the staffs themselves, and partly and more recently to joint organization of both the staffs and the Local Authorities in Whitley machinery for collective bargaining. Despite the enormous variety of professions and occupations comprised within the Local Government Service, its members have achieved the remarkable feat of establishing one Trade Union which caters for them all (except the manual workers). This organization was originally called the National Association of Local Government Officers, but is now styled the National and Local Government Officers Association (with the same short title 'Nalgo.'); and all members of the professional, technical, administrative, and clerical staffs of the Local Authorities are eligible to join it—from Town Clerks down to office boys. So comprehensive an organization (in strong contrast to the Unions which cater for the separated layers of the Civil Service) is believed to be unique in Trade Union structure throughout the world. It is not for the author to discuss the merits of this organization here, except to notice that it has consistently taken a very broad view of its functions as a Trade Union and pursued a whole-hearted and vigorous policy of raising the qualifications and standards of service of all Local Government Officers. It has also sought to pursue all its objects through the machinery of Whitleyism, i.e. standing machinery of collective negotiation jointly established by the employers and employees, to regulate the relations between them.

In the early years the Association's policy was justifiably preoccupied with endeavours to improve the pay of the clerical grades, and to gain a compulsory superannuation scheme for the Service as a whole—which latter object it achieved with the passing of the Local Government Superannuation Act in 1937. Even these endeavours did much to raise the efficiency of the Service; for there can be little doubt that grading schemes and superannuation have improved mobility in the Service and opened up promotion to younger and better equipped men. After the 1914 war, the Association managed to get its policy of Whitleyism adopted by the Local Authorities in certain of the provinces; and prior to or soon after the outbreak of the 1939 war Provincial Whitley Councils had established themselves throughout the country, and had formulated provincial grading schemes and standard conditions of service. For many years, however, Whitleyism in the Local Government Service lacked its most important element: a National Joint Council. Such a Council had been inaugurated soon after the 1914-18 war, but, for reasons which we need not detail here, very soon collapsed. It was revived just before the war of 1939, but lacked influence and strength because it failed to secure the blessing of the Local Authority Associations. For one reason and another, the 1939 war gave a considerable impetus to Nalgo's policy of full Local Authority support for Whitley machinery; but the Local Authority Associations, pressed to give their support, found impediments in certain aspects of the National Joint Council's constitution. After protracted negotiations during the war these impediments were at last removed; and in 1944 a new National Council came into being to which the Local Authority Associations felt able to accord full support; and on which, in fact, they are now directly represented. In 1946 the Council approved a national scheme of salaries and service conditions, known as 'the charter', providing a framework of scales for the grading of posts. This is now operative throughout the country and it has in part been supplemented by agreements for standard gradings among certain classes of officer. More recently still special negotiating committees have agreed upon scales of pay and standard conditions of service for the Chief Officers of Local Authorities who fall outside the National Joint Council's purview.

From the first Nalgo was prepared to let Whitley machinery deal also with questions of recruitment, training, and qualification. Questions of this kind were reviewed by the Hadow Departmental Committee in 1934; but that Committee rejected the idea of dealing with them through Whitley machinery and advocated the establishment of an *ad hoc* body representative of the Local Authorities, the staffs, and certain other agencies. Certain of the Local Authority Associations were at that time willing neither to set up machinery of the kind recommended by the Hadow Committee nor to let the existing Whitley machinery handle this question. With the removal of the constitutional impediments which stood in the way of the Local Authority Associations' support for the National Joint Council, and the rehabilitation of that body, the Local Authorities turned in favour of bringing such questions within the jurisdiction of the Whitley machinery.

It has been said that neither employers nor employees should be left entirely free to settle the qualifications of a service such as the Local Government Service, since these qualifications must obviously influence, if indeed they do not determine, the standard of service to the public. It has also been contended that the atmosphere of Whitleyism is essentially one of bargaining, and that questions of qualification and training cannot fittingly be left to the higgling of the market, or to the play of compromise and expediency which enters into industrial negotiation. On the other hand, the interests of employers and employees, though not the only ones, are the principal ones from a practical standpoint, and it is natural that they should both desire to retain in their own hands any collective machinery which deals with qualification and recruitment. Moreover, their agreement is essential to any policy in matters of this kind which is not imposed by the State—and the State is hardly likely to wish to interfere in so wide a field as this. Finally, both parties now take the view that standards of recruitment, training, and qualification are indissolubly linked with standards of pay and service conditions; and since Whitley machinery has dealt, and must continue to deal with the latter, it has an obvious claim to handle the former.

In such a situation, the practical policy soon became clear when it was agreed to reconstitute the National Joint Council. The Whitley machinery must be the mechanism for settling standards of recruitment, training and qualification; but it must make special arrangements to deal with them. It must remove them, at any rate in the first instance, from the ordinary processes of bargaining. It must enlist the advice of outside agencies, such as the Universities, the governing bodies of the professions, and the various occupational groups of the service, upon the standards to be adopted.

Such a policy has now been implemented by the National Joint Council, through the establishment, under its auspices, of a Local Government Examinations Board, which is also charged with advisory functions on questions of education, qualification, and training.

The report of the Hadow Departmental Committee was the last authoritative survey of the conditions relating to recruitment, training, and qualification in the Local Government Service, and it admittedly found much room for improvement, chiefly in the clerical grades. It must be remembered, however, that since then Nalgo's policy of improvement has been ever more active and fruitful, that first the Provincial and now the National Joint Whitley Councils have been firmly established in the local government system and done a vast amount of work, and that the employers' representatives on the Whitley Councils have on the whole made common cause with the staffs' organizations in looking for the highest standards of service and qualifications. The national scheme of service conditions imposes standards of recruitment for clerical staff and Promotion Examinations, and makes provision for post-entry educational facilities. The Local Government Examinations Board has introduced a Clerical Division Examination and a syllabus and examinations for a Diploma in Municipial Administration. The National Joint Council has also encouraged the recruitment of university graduates. There is now an increasing flow of officers with university qualifications (or the equivalents provided by the Examinations Board), often in addition to the professional qualifications which Chief Officers and the higher grades must possess as a *sine qua non*.

There is always room for improvement in these matters; but some of the pictures painted by outside commentators writing many years ago of the low standards of recruitment to the Local Government Service can safely be regarded as overdrawn, or out of date. The new Whitley agencies have done much to exterminate nepotism in recruitment and appointment, and to secure more satisfactory standards of entry to the basic clerical grades; and Nalgo's policy of higher occupational education for senior as well as junior staff has been bearing good fruit for many years now. The recruitment to the basic grades is not yet as orderly in the Local Government Service as it is in the Civil Service; but the educational differences are not what they used to be in the last century. The consciousness of early deficiencies has stimulated the Local Government Service to post-entry training on a scale which far exceeds that which is prevalent in the Civil Service. The younger officers—including many who possess the essential professional qualifications, and will be the Chief Officers of tomorrow—have been noticeably alive to the need for occupational training of the broader kind in administrative and social subjects.

There is nothing in the Local Government Service today, or in the requirements the country may make upon it tomorrow, which calls for any radically different basis of organization. In particular, there appears to be little warrant for the suggestion that it needs to form a segregated Administrative Class of the kind known to the Civil Service. Once the remaining scars of nepotism are removed, by the highly developed professional sense of the young officers of today, as well as by Whitley

I

agencies, and provided the tests agreed in the Charter are maintained, the principles on which the Local Government Service is recruited and trained may be shown to have not a few advantages over those of the Civil Service.

The principal difference between the two Services is in the character of the qualifications and training required for the controlling grades. In the Local Government Service, departmental heads and their chief assistants are men of professional training and experience (and often of supplementary vocational training) who have acquired administrative experience and reputation in moving up the ladder of promotion. In the Civil Service, officers of the administrative class are recruited principally from the older Universities on the basis of high academic achievement; and they assume their administrative responsibilities after serving as cadets and carrying out minor administrative duties without any vocational training. Professional and technical grades are employed in the Civil Service, but usually as a subordinate class. So rigid has been the philosophy which led to the establishment of the administrative class that it has been almost impossible for those in the professional grades to pass over to administrative rank and become departmental chiefs or assistant chiefs.

This arrangement is based on the view that the essential factor for responsible administrative work is the broad, openminded, but critical mentality induced by a liberal education on the usual academic lines. The trained mind is beyond all doubt the best raw material of administrative ability; but is the purely academic way the only way of securing it? The philosophy which informs the recruitment of the administrative class in the Civil Service assumes what, today, those who rightly stress the value of a liberal education would never claim, i.e. that education for a learned profession cannot be a liberal education, or that a professional training cannot develop broad mental approach and resource, but only rule-of-thumb competence in a narrow sphere. Yet only a few years ago the Spens Committee on Secondary Education expressed the view that even technical education, orientated as it can be today, can be a liberal education in the fullest sense!

It is, of course, common ground that no amount of mental training will make an administrator if certain qualities of temperament and character, and a modicum of mother-wit, are missing; and the true comparison between the two Services in this respect lies in the extent to which they detect and develop these qualities. We have already said something on this score in Chapter VI, and there is no need to pursue the topic here, except to say that the Local Government Service does not appear to disadvantage on this issue. The fact we wish to stress here is that public administration today calls even more insistently for specific occupational knowledge. It is no longer safe to rely upon the light of nature, however fortified by high academic achievement, as the test of administrative competence; or to leave much that is of any importance to those processes of trial and error by which the administrative cadets of the Civil Service acquire their experience—the Civil Service having until quite recently failed, as a White Paper of 1944 admitted, to set up any proper arrangements for training them.

The professional and occupational training of the local government administrator shows to advantage in the light of these considerations. Nearly all the professional qualifications of Local Government Officers contribute in one direction or another to the fund of knowledge which is an essential background to administrative activity; and in these days professional bodies are giving increasing weight and scope to sections of their syllabus which provide a background knowledge of the kind specifically required for the public service. Moreover, as already mentioned, many of the supplementary qualifications of Local Government Officers are entirely related to public administration.

Two further advantages accrue to the local government administrator in the early professional training and experience which the Service requires of him. He starts responsible work earlier; and thus becomes acclimatized to responsibility, initiative, and discretion, in his formative years. By the time an administrative officer in the Civil Service is emerging from the cadet grade, a professional officer in the Local Government Service, or a professional man who subsequently enters it and progresses to administrative responsibilities, has already undertaken a large variety of responsible jobs; and, not least important, become acquainted with men and affairs. Secondly, in local government the employer takes the view that the head of a department must be more than nominally responsible for the department's work; and feels that if the head is to have such a real responsibility for professional and technical work he must know something about it. Local Authorities insist upon responsibility being real and visible, and think it an advantage that a man supervising professional men shall know about their work and thus know how to organize it, and how to settle and adjust a staff establishment with understanding.

There is one further great difference between the two bodies. The Civil Servant is in the unified employment of the Crown. The Local Government Officer serves a particular Local Authority. The Civil Servant may move from place to place; but he moves under one employment, one code of test, and one promotion system, and with no direct outside tests of his ability. The Local Government Officer, having acquired pre-requisite qualifications and experience in the field enters into a competitive market, and normally submits himself to the inspection, not of one, but of many testing agencies. The nature of his job and visibility of his responsibilities ensure that, though he may bluff for a time, he can never bluff for long. Sooner or later his Council and his town find his measure, and he passes for what he is worth. His reputation becomes known in the local government world at large. These stimulating conditions might well perish in a unified Service. By all means let the Service move, through Whitleyism, towards basic uniformities in grading, in the way it has already achieved uniform scales of salary, and towards standards of qualification and training; but let it preserve the officer's independent contract with his Authority and the competitive mobility which subjects him to successive and varied tests and stimulates his initiative.

There are two other features of Local Government Service which tend to strengthen the Local Government Officer's administrative capacity as compared with that of the Civil Servant; his intimate collaboration, under the municipal system, with the public and their representatives; and the field experience in which he sees public administration brought to its final test. Differences of this kind, however, spring from the different systems of Parliamentary and municipal government, already referred to in Chapter VI.

The foregoing observations and arguments do not rest on the view that the Local Government Service is superior in calibre to the Civil Service, or on the view that the Local Government

Service is yet what it ought to be; but on the view that if well recognized defects in the Local Government Service can be removed, the system on which it is built up has its own merits and some advantages and that the Civil Service is not a model to be slavishly copied in the work of local government.

DEPARTMENTAL STRUCTURE

In Boroughs and Districts the number of major departments will not usually exceed four, namely, the Clerk's, the Treasurer's, the Engineer and Surveyor's, and the Health and/or Public Health Inspector's; plus Trading Departments—Water or Transport—according to the Local Authority's responsibilities in this sphere. In the larger Authorities, particularly the County Boroughs, the departments may number as many as sixteen or more. The table in Appendix C shows the departmental lay-out of an average County Borough and the broad categories of staff engaged in each department.

The departmental lay-out shown in this table exhibits a fairly high degree of integration, by which term I mean a grouping of several functions or classes of work into one departmental sphere. As a general rule it is desirable to integrate as much as possible. The number of departments is thus reduced to a minimum, and inter-departmental co-ordination rendered easier. There are no doubt certain officers, not quite of the standing of the statutory officers or the heads of major services, whose functions may be specialized, who require little supervision, who can be allowed considerable freedom to work independently, and whom it would be possible to leave as independent officers. Nevertheless, it is usually better to integrate so as to attach them to some major department whose chief functions are not too dissimilar to their own. Such a course will eliminate the tendency, natural enough, for officers of this kind to build up departments of their own, and in meeting their needs for typing and clerical staff out of the broader departmental resources will usually do so no less effectively and usually more economically.

But the extent to which integration can go will be found to vary very considerably with the type and size of the individual Authority. Thus, in the table shown, architectural work (including housing) and control of sewage works lie within the ambit of the Engineer and Surveyor's Department; and for a place of moderate size this is certainly better than having a separate Architect's Department and leaving sewage disposal under an independent officer. On the other hand, though in small Authorities it would be found preferable to include in the Surveyor's Department the Parks Superintendent, Cemetery Superintendent, and Cleansing and Lighting Officers, rather than leave them as independent officers, they are shown as chiefs of separate departments in the table; and in a County Borough of average size this is usual and preferable.

In very small authorities no great harm may be done if specialist officers are left with independent responsibility to the Council direct, if each has no considerable need for clerical or routine staff, and if the Clerk is exercising a personal supervision over other officers, as in small authorities he often does. But in the vast majority of cases a strong presumption in favour of integration is operative, particularly as the natural trend, on a balance of considerations, is usually in the other direction. Nevertheless, there is an upper limit of size beyond which integration cannot go, and needs arise in the reverse direction. Thus the large cities have found the need for a separate Architect's Department, a separate Housing Department, or a separate Estates Department, and in the pressure of housing work the larger towns are having to resort to a similar arrangement. There are many considerations which determine the point of departure, but generally speaking it is reached when there is no further economy or convenience to be gained by integrating routine and clerical work in the wider department, while advantage will accrue from more specialized knowledge and experience 'at the top' for each of the functions to be separated.

DEPARTMENTAL CO-ORDINATION

Co-ordination in the work of the Local Authority depends on a number of factors best looked at on the planes of policy and of administration respectively, though factors mainly affecting policy may also affect administration, and vice-versa.

The main factors contributing to co-ordination of policy are a good layout of committees and careful attention to finance, in both its general and particular aspects, through effective machinery for budgetary procedure and budgetary control.

These we have already considered. A potent and beneficial effect in co-ordinating policy is also claimed to be one of the virtues of the party system in local government, and the claim is, in the author's view, a valid one.

Administrative co-ordination, which is what we are mainly concerned with in this book, rests firstly on organizational structure and secondly on the day-to-day co-ordination effected by Management in its dynamic aspect. It is usually the second which is emphasised, and, indeed, mostly thought of when the word co-ordination is mentioned, but it is the first of the two factors which is the more important and has the greatest effect. The very aim of organization, indeed, is to make such a division of labour as will facilitate and maximize *self*-co-ordination, among organic groups in the structure, and among individuals. Whether this self-co-ordination is in fact achieved will depend on the staff's knowledge of their place and function in the structure, and their relationships with others. In terms of municipal organization, the structure mostly concerned is the Departmental structure, though Committee-structure too bears on administrative co-ordination as well as co-ordination of policy. All, then, that we have said on these two topics is of direct relevance in considering the roots of administrative co-ordination.

Nevertheless, when everything is achieved through structure that can be achieved there does remain a sphere for the day-to-day activity of Management—for the personal activity of the co-ordinator. How is co-ordination of this kind effected?

The short answer is: 'Through the Clerk.' It can never be achieved, however, merely by virtue of the office which the Clerk holds. Conscious and special effort is necessary if it is to be achieved in any adequate measure; and although in recent years, as the Local Authorities' range of services has widened more and more, efforts have been made by many Local Authorities to strengthen the Clerk's powers to co-ordinate other officers, no universally recognized ways and means of doing so have evolved as yet. Certain elementary processes of co-ordination do arise out of the Clerk's duties as recipient of the Council's correspondence. It is for him to decide to what departments any communication should be referred, either for attention or for report, either to him, or to the committee concerned if a committee decision is required. If the matter con-

cerns more than one department, or the task is new, it is for
him to analyse the departmental activity involved and arrange
for the necessary co-operation or consultation. It is obvious,
however, that co-ordination must go further than this; and that
if the Clerk is to co-ordinate he must be enabled to call upon
the departments for action on his own initiative, and to take
the initiative in bringing their advice or resources to bear upon
some executive need or problem; and must have power to ex-
amine and review the major mechanisms of the administrative
machine and in particular the liaisons between all departments.

Functions of this kind require authority; and it is for this
reason that Authorities now designate their Clerks as Chief
Administrative and Executive Officers. Yet even this course
does not automatically solve all problems. To some officers such
as the Surveyor or the Medical Officer of Health or Public
Health Inspector statute often speaks directly, giving them
individual directions and responsibilities of their own; and
nothing the Council or the Clerk can do can relieve those
officers of individual responsibilities such as these. This circumstance alone prevents the Clerk from occupying a position of
concentrated authority and responsibility such as that occupied
by the Managing Director in business. Again, it cannot be
expected that over the wide range of a modern Local
Authority's work any one man can assume even a nominal
responsibility for the executive work of all the departments.
The Departmental Heads, by deep-rooted practice, have executive responsibility for the working of their own departments.
Nominally, a Managing Director does assume the wider kind of
responsibility, though it is to be doubted whether the situation
is really as different in the two cases as it looks. Can a Managing
Director really assume responsibility for the work of his highly
specialized or technical subordinates? can he on issues of a
technical or specialist character effectually interfere with them,
or reject their advice? Broadly, the appropriate function of the
principal officer in both cases is to assume a general supervision,
the oversight of the general character of the administrative
arrangement and organization and general co-ordination.

It is functions of this latter kind which Clerks are coming
to assume. How, in fact, are they enabled to exercise them
under the procedure of a Local Authority? At departmental
level, it is for the Clerk to lay down, preferably with the sup-

port of Standing Orders, a machinery of consultation on certain matters. If he is the Legal Officer, as is almost invariably the case, this is the more easily done, because there must of necessity be established some understanding as to the matters, the occasions, and the times when resort to him is necessary in legal matters, and there should be no difficulty in procuring a similar type of authorization in administrative matters. The real opportunity for the exercise of co-ordinating functions, however, lies at committee level; for here, as we have so often reiterated in other connections, all business of more than managerial nature must eventually arrive. At this level the Clerk can exercise a co-ordinative function by tendering his observations on the reports of the departmental heads, without in any way fettering their responsibility to speak their own minds in their reports, or relieving them from any responsibility they possess on the executive side. In view of this situation it is more than ever important that the reports of departmental heads should be circulated in advance to committees and to the Clerk. By Standing Order the Clerk should be given the power, and, where uniformity of practice, questions of co-ordination, or (where the Clerk is also the Legal Officer) questions of law, are concerned, he should be placed under the duty of tendering his observations to the committee. The atmosphere of committee is, or ought to be, a friendly one. With his right to report according to his own views and discretion left fully safeguarded, no departmental head should feel disturbed by observations put forward on his report by the Clerk. If time permits, and on matters of importance, the Clerk's observations should be issued, as should the departmental heads' reports, in written form, and in advance.

CHAPTER IX

The Reorganization of Local Authorities

THE NEED FOR REFORM

THERE ARE many reasons why the structure of local government is to-day in acute need of reform. But the root cause of trouble is that we still retain a pattern of local authorities fashioned, in essence, in the closing years of the nineteenth century when the tasks borne by local councils were far fewer and far less complex than in contemporary Britain. We noted in Chapter II the main principles that provide the basis of the present structure. The application of these principles led to the establishment of a number of small authorities of uneconomic size and inadequate resources, for this was the inevitable consequence of an urban-rural differentiation which marks out as a separate unit any small urban community too big to be left as a parish. They produced, in the County areas, a division of functions, and sometimes of responsibilities in the same service, which had the serious consequences divided responsibility can have in any sphere, and which has in any event rendered co-operation difficult. Outside County Boroughs they permitted, as an administrative unit for the larger services, Counties whose boundaries are unsuitable, which frequently fail to weld their mixed urban and rural elements into real communities, which are based on old county towns unsuitably placed as seats of government, and which suffer from the vices of remote control. And there has now grown up, it is widely argued, a need in some services for areas transcending any of the present units.

It is essential to realize, however, before we entirely condemn the present structure, that many of its defects arise not from the plan it embodies, but from the misapplication of this plan in practice. The misapplications of the plan have sprung from three sources—first, extensive preservations of existing status and privilege at each successive stage in the growth of the structure; secondly, the makeshift lines upon which new functions have been distributed among the Local Authorities; and thirdly, the lack of sufficiently responsive machinery for the adaptation of the structure to changing conditions of population and development, and for the adjustment of the Local Authorities' status, boundaries and functions. Let us review these factors in turn.

There was a noticeable instance of the preservation of old forms in the very beginnings of the modern system. On the passing of the Municipal Corporations Act in 1835 the ancient chartered Corporations, consisting largely of towns of pre-industrial revolution size, were for the most part only re-formed, not abolished. Boroughs of 2,000-5,000 are thought by most people to be uneconomically small and incapable of financing or staffing services of the kind they must now perform; why should they still remain? But perhaps the most striking instance of the preservation of old forms was the adoption in 1888 of the geographical Counties (with the few modifications already noted) as the new large-scale units outside the County Boroughs.

The second factor has produced a chronic state of maladjustment in the incidence of functions upon individual local authorities; and it is important to notice how it has operated. The powers initially accruing to the Councils in the Acts which established them have often been but slight; and most of the powers possessed at present have been obtained by Councils, after their establishment, through General Acts dealing comprehensively with a particular service. The pace of social legislation has been so great that there has been no time to make any judicious selection, on the basis of local circumstances, of the particular authorities best able to support and conduct the services in a given area. The policy generally followed has been to decide broadly whether the service should be given to the authorities supposed to be large, or to those supposed to be small—which means the Counties and the County Boroughs on the one hand and the Boroughs and Districts on the other. In point of fact, not all Counties are really large, and not all the Boroughs and Districts are small.

Moreover, as we have seen, there are striking divergences of size and resources in each class of authorities. It is obvious that the distribution of powers upon an 'automatic' footing in the way described could not be otherwise than anomalous and unsatisfactory. Services have been given to some of the small Boroughs and Districts which they could not adequately maintain. In contrast, services have sometimes been given to the County Council which could better have been given, for the sake of closer local interest and control, more convenient and sometimes less expensive management, to a Borough or Urban District of substantial size, well capable of sustaining the responsibility.

Sometimes the distribution of powers in this 'automatic' way has been tempered by conferring powers upon Boroughs and Districts attaining a prescribed population-level, while leaving the smaller Boroughs and Districts to be catered for by the County. Thus, while the Education Act of 1902 made the County Council responsible for secondary education throughout the County, it allowed elementary education to be undertaken by Boroughs if over 10,000 population, and by Urban Districts if over 20,000. This system ended in 1944. Arrangements of a similar type still apply to the administration of the Food and Drugs, Weights and Measures, Diseases of Animals, and Explosives Acts, and of the Milk and Dairies Orders. The distribution of functions on a population basis is now used in conjunction with the device of delegation; non-county Boroughs and County Districts with a population above 60,000 commonly operate delegated powers in respect of education, planning, health and welfare services. The tendency since 1944 has been to redistribute functions to the top-tier County authorities but to pacify medium-sized towns by giving them delegated powers. Local government reform has come about by reshaping the administration of individual services and not by clear sighted reorganisation of the structure as a whole.

Since the end of the last century there have been great changes in the distribution of our population and of its behaviour and requirements. These changes have been stimulated by technical advances, especially the development of electric power and the invention of the petrol engine. Both of these have exerted major influence on industrial location and town development. The availability of electric power everywhere has meant that industry need no longer confine itself to the precincts of existing towns, to a siting on coal-fields, or to places chosen mainly with an eye on railway communications.

Motor transport has furnished industry with additional or alternative facilities for bringing in raw materials or marketing the finished product, and has opened up residence well beyond the existing towns. There has been a large shift of industry and population from the older industrial areas of the North to the South. An outspread of population from nearly all the towns has resulted in 'suburban sprawl' or 'overspill'. New towns or new 'built-up areas' have appeared in areas formerly rural. Shifts and movements of this kind have caused neighbouring towns to coalesce, or virtually joined them together by intervening 'development'. In some areas they have combined to produce those huge agglomerations or urban populations we now call conurbations—of which there are six—Greater London (by far the largest, with a population of 8½ million), Tyneside, West Yorkshire, South-East Lancashire, Merseyside and West Midlands.

In terms of Local Government structure this has meant that new defects in the layout of areas have accrued on top of the old, creating further anomalies in status, as well as in size and the distribution of functions. County Boroughs have over-spilled into rural areas; some Rural Districts have become predominantly urban in character; some parishes have grown larger than many Urban Districts; some towns have merged together in areas of continuous urban development but retain separate local government units; many non-County Boroughs have grown substantially larger than the smaller County Boroughs; and many diminutive units 'saved' under earlier legislation are by modern standards and requirements more diminutive than ever. Examples of the foregoing can be found throughout the country, but nowhere is the need for change more acute than in the conurbations.

Finally, the plan of 1888-1894 has gone awry through failure to keep it adjusted to these changes in the distribution of population and the growth and decline of communities. Until 1929, changes in the status and boundaries of local authorities rested almost entirely on their own initiative in procedure for Provisional Orders or Local Private Acts. As substantial shifts in population set in after the turn of the century, Parliament became the battle-ground for the opposing interests of Counties and County Boroughs in moves by the County Boroughs to extend their boundaries, or by growing

Boroughs for County Borough status. Alterations affecting the smaller Boroughs and the Districts depended on the initiative and attitude of the County Councils; and little change in fact took place. The boundaries of the Counties themselves, except as affected by extensions of County Borough boundaries, or by the very small number of new County Boroughs which were in fact created, remained immune from change, or even scrutiny.

In this situation the Local Government Act of 1929 made some improvement by inaugurating ten-yearly general reviews of County District areas by the County Councils ('County Reviews'); but did nothing much to resolve the conflict between Counties and County Boroughs or to rationalise County boundaries. The first review under the Act of 1929 was duly completed, but although it accomplished something useful it is now generally admitted that its impact on the situation as a whole was not very great. The second review, due in 1939, was postponed on the outbreak of war.

PROPOSALS FOR REFORM

Before 1939 the discussion of local government structure was largely confined to those actively concerned with local administration, but the period of the Second World War brought about a remarkable change. The topic came under discussion in wider circles, and was claimed to be an urgent practical problem. There were several reasons which brought it to the forefront. Some difficulty had been experienced in adapting the structure to the requirements of Civil Defence. War-time tasks had thrown some of the general defects of the system into clear relief, and it was feared that these might become major impediments to a speedy onslaught upon the tasks of reconstruction. Further, as the Government began to develop a programme of post-war social legislation, it was assumed that much of this would be administered through the agency of local government; so it was necessary to see that its machinery could be adapted to such new tasks. Accordingly, most of the organized bodies concerned with local government appointed committees of inquiry to re-examine the question of local government structure; and by 1943 or thereabouts most of these bodies had published their views.

All of them, without exception, expressed a strong feeling against any continuation of the system of Regional Commissioners established during the war, or any similar system of regional control by Government Departments; and most of them argued that local government required no such extensive new unit for normal purposes. They all upheld the compendious principle of organization, and pointed out the danger of a reversion to *ad hoc* authorities if the structure was reformed piecemeal to accommodate the needs now of this service and now of that. They all urged, on the contrary, that a general system of compendious local authorities should be retained, adapted to the requirements of local government as a whole; and considered it to be the Government's duty to measure the total impact, upon the present structure, of any new services to be entrusted to local authorities, or of any developments in existing services which called for different areas or different types of authority. Thus far there was common ground among the organizations which considered the future of local government.

In all other respects the measure of agreement was slight. With one exception, the Local Authority Associations took the view that no great changes were required in the present system. The Association of Municipal Corporations, after some internal dissension, did put forward a plan for a new structure, as also did the Labour Party and a Reconstruction Committee appointed by the National and Local Government Officers Association (Nalgo). But the solutions put forward by these three bodies were very different.

The schemes of the A.M.C., the Labour Party and Nalgo each recognized that some services need wider areas than single Counties or County Boroughs. The Association of Municipal Corporations' scheme did not precisely say what services of this kind it had in mind; but the other two schemes were more definite. The Labour Party placed the overwhelming majority of existing services in this category. The Nalgo scheme mentioned town and country planning, public health and public assistance, hospitals and institutions, major highway developments, provision for specialist and technical education, main drainage and sewage disposal, provincial library provision, and public utility services. In looking at these schemes today it should be appreciated that the hospital service, and gas and electricity supply, have been taken outside the scope of local government, and that in these three fields the case for wide areas was strongest.

The A.M.C. scheme advocated a structure based uniformly on a single compendious ('all-purposes') authority in all areas. This was an ideal put forward by John Stuart Mill in the middle of the last century, but only partly realized in the existing structure. The A.M.C. favoured it because they were impressed with the virtues of the County Borough and with the defects, in the way of divided responsibilities and imperfect co-ordination, of the three-tier system in the County. Unassailable as the full compendious form of organization may be in large though compact urban areas, it may nevertheless be doubted whether the compendious principle can be carried into large areas of different or diverse character. If it be true that some services require handling over areas which will transcend the Counties and the County Boroughs, then these will manifestly be very large if they are to have single all-purposes authorities and will bring extensive urban and rural areas into the same unit. The very size of such an area will mean a deterioration of local interest and control wherever there is a well-marked local community. It may also be doubted whether, over the large areas which the plan involved, urban and rural communities can be successfully blended. Modern transport notwithstanding, there are still many diversities of interest in urban and rural communities, and very great differences of outlook. Is there much common aim or interest in a large industrial city and rural territory, say, twenty miles from it? Is either likely to be better served than if it concentrated on its own problems with suitable machinery for co-operation? If expenditure in each all-purposes areas is to be pooled, as seems necessary, a marriage of urban and rural elements may add money-quarrels to incompatibility of temperament, for there can be no formula for uniform expenditure in urban and rural places. Despite much loose talk about serving the country in the same way as the town, their needs vary considerably.

The Labour Party's scheme was on different lines and favoured a two-tier structure, comprising a series of directly elected Regional Councils to handle the large-scale services and a series of directly elected Area Councils to handle the small-scale services. In an earlier version of the proposals it was suggested that there should be 40 Regional Authorities and about 150 Area Authorities, and the average size of the latter therefore works out at about 250,000 to 300,000 population. There seems little doubt that the Regional areas would, like the areas contemplated by the A.M.C., comprise extensive tracts of rural as well as urban territory, and the arrangement would therefore attract the same criticisms as the proposals of the A.M.C. On the other hand, second-tier areas of 250,000 to 300,000 population level, whose Councils would handle the comparatively minor functions allocated to them in the schedule to the scheme, would insulate local government as a whole from all vital local interest, contact and control. This scheme is now mainly of historical interest for the Labour Party has since lost enthusiasm for any drastic changes in local government.

The Nalgo Committee's Report (which represented the views of an independent committee and not the official policy of the Association), put forward a scheme which sought to meet the same major aims as the other two but in a markedly different way. Like the A.M.C scheme, it recognized the impressive virtues of the compendious principle as applied fully in the County Borough of today. Thus it proposed that the primary unit of local government should be a single all-purpose authority. It recognised, however, that the services mentioned above need to be planned over larger areas. In the analysis of the situation made by the Nalgo Committee's Report the need is not so much for these services to be *administered* over 'outsize' areas, as for them to be *planned* over such areas. For this purpose it proposed, while recognising the defects which mark indirectly elected bodies, that Provincial Councils indirectly elected by groups of all-purposes authorities should do the planning; while the all-purposes authorities, of about 100,000 to 250,000 population (or of higher levels in the big cities), should administer these services, and of course both plan and administer all the other services not requiring special treatment of this kind. In a word, the Provincial Councils would be scheme-making authorities whose schemes were eventually made binding by central approval. A further feature of the Nalgo scheme was that, while administration would be unitary in the compact

K

administrative areas similar to the County Borough of today, District Councils or Committees would be set up for each well-recognised local community in the all-purposes administrative areas of mixed population characteristics, and these would exercise a substantial range of delegated power from the administrative authority. The existing smaller Boroughs and Urban Districts could be fitted into a system of delegation of this kind and would thus preserve their identity as communities, though they would lose the autonomous authority they possess today.

After refusing for a long time to make any comprehensive inquiry into the matter, still less to declare its own mind upon the subject, the Government eventually published, in the early part of 1945, a White Paper entitled 'Local Government in England and Wales during the period of Reconstruction' (Cmd. 6579), putting forward the Government's policy in the matter. In this the Government, after repudiating any intention to perpetuate the system of Regional Commissioners, declared that it saw no need, at any rate in the immediate post-war period, for any different structure, but expressed itself as 'satisfied that within the general framework of the County and County Borough system there is need and scope for improvements, and in particular for amending the machinery of the Local Government Act 1933 relating to adjustments of status, boundaries and areas.' In any event, to attempt to create any new structure would, the Government pointed out, seriously impede local government in its immediate post-war tasks, particularly in dealing with the new measures for Education and a comprehensive Health Service. It would take a long time to settle what new plan should be introduced and still longer to erect a new structure, and transfer the tasks of local government from the old structure to the new. These arguments undoubtedly carried weight, even with advocates of radical reform, and there was wide agreement that we should not disrupt the existing machine or leave existing authorities with an uncertain future hanging over them at a time when local government would be called upon for its maximum effort. The White Paper recognized, with an air of reluctance and doubt, that there might be some services which need areas transcending the limits of a single County or County Borough; but to meet the needs of such services it proposed to resort to the not unfamiliar devices of a Joint Committee or a Joint Board. The White Paper also noted the number of diminutive authorities and agreed with the view that they are hardly equal to the responsibilities of modern local government. It admitted that the machinery for readjusting the structure to changed conditions had been too slow and faulty in the past, and it adopted the idea of a standing Boundary Commission—which was put forward in the Report of the Nalgo Reconstruction Committee—as the best instrument for achieving this end. The Boundary Commission should have executive powers to alter the status, area and boundaries of local authorities of all kinds, subject in some instances to parliamentary and ministerial safeguards. County boundaries should no longer be immune from a process of systematic periodical review, and the powers of the County Council to review the status and boundaries of County Districts should pass to the Commission. London and Middlesex did not come within the scope of the Boundary Commission, as the Government considered that conditions there gave rise to special problems. The project of a Boundary Commission met with general agreement in local government circles, but many of those who thought it best not to disrupt the existing structure in the first post-war years felt that radical changes could not long be delayed.

Parliament subsequently passed the Local Government (Boundary Commission) Act, 1945, establishing the Commission and giving it directions which enabled it to alter the local authorities' areas and, within the limits of the existing system, to change their status. Alterations to Counties or County Boroughs, including decisions to create new County Boroughs or to down-grade existing ones, needed Parliamentary confirmation. The Commission was not empowered to create units of a new type, nor did the Act itself provide for the creation of any new kind of authority. In their second Report, for 1947, they presented the results of their investigation of the position throughout the country. They drew attention to new features which had entered into their task since their appointment—the transfer of many services to the State and of responsibilities from Boroughs and Districts to the County. In effect, they intimated that the situation could not be dealt with everywhere by re-applying the same kind of units as those which exist today. After discussing the broad alternatives which they found to lie before them—largely turning, as one might expect, on the issue of one-tier or two-tier government —they submitted their own proposals for a change in system.

Apart from the absence of any proposals for regionalism, the Commissioners' proposals were radical. They wished to confine one-tier government to the largest cities. Not all of these were chosen and there would only be 17 in all: Birmingham, Bradford, Bristol, Coventry, Derby, Hull, Leeds, Leicester, Newcastle, Nottingham, Plymouth, Portsmouth, Sheffield, Southampton, Stafford North (a new Potteries unit), Sunderland and Sussex Central (a new unit to be formed by combining Brighton, Hove and district). These, or the nucleus of them, are today County Boroughs; but the Commissioners proposed to give them the name of 'one-tier Counties'. The rest of the country, including the Manchester and Liverpool conurbations, was to come under a new two-tier system. This was to be based on a division of the country into newly shaped Counties with a minimum population of 200,000, existing small Counties being eliminated and the largest subdivided,— Lancashire into as many as five. Within the Counties there would be reshaped Boroughs, Urban Districts and Rural Districts, the powers of the two latter being assimilated, also a number of larger town units retaining the style 'County Borough' but being something different from the County Boroughs of today. The new class of County Boroughs would have all powers except for planning, police, fire service and main roads; consequently Health and Education would be re-transferred to them from the counties. In 'two-tier' Counties there would be a major re-shuffle of responsibilities. Most of the existing County Boroughs, i.e. those not becoming one-tier Counties, would lose functions and in effect be down-graded. Even Manchester and Liverpool were put forward for inclusion in this class, apparently because they were regarded as parts of a conurbation in some sense that Birmingham was not. On the other hand, many of the existing Non-County Boroughs would step up into this new type of County Borough for which the population limits, apart from Liverpool and Manchester, were put forward at 60,000 to 200,000.

The reaction of the Government to the Commission's second report was as drastic as it was in most quarters unexpected. Parliament was asked to repeal the 1945 Act and to wind up the Commission. Both objects were effected by the Local Government Boundary Commission (Dissolution) Act, 1949. The Government never explained its initiative in any great detail, but indicated clearly enough that the Commission's proposals were unacceptable. It also announced that it was itself reviewing the structure and functions of local government but could hold out no prospect of immediate legislation.

In 1953 the topic was revived when the Conservative Government invited the associations of local authorities to consider the issues anew and see whether any measure of agreement among them might now be forthcoming. The County Borough and the County authorities at first registered again their advocacy of the one-tier and two-tier solutions respectively; but on the Government informing them that it was 'not prepared to eliminate either the two-tier system in the Counties or the one-tier system in the big towns', they reached a measure of agreement, notably on the need for a Local Government Commission to review areas and status, and on a norm of 100,000 population for eligibility for County Borough status, except in conurbations where it should be 125,000. As between the County and County District authorities, a measure of agreement was reached on the distribution of functions within the County, and on categories of functions which should or could be delegated from Counties to Districts.

In 1956 the Government announced its conclusion that 'there is no convincing case for radically re-shaping the existing forms of local government and that what is needed is to overhaul it and make such improvements as are necessary to bring it up to date'. The measures decided upon to this end were set out in a White Paper Cmd. 9831 of July 1956 entitled 'Areas and Status of Local Authorities in England and Wales'. A further White Paper, Cmnd. 161 of May 1957 entitled 'Functions of County Councils and County District Councils in England and Wales' reviewed the distribution of functions in the County areas, expressed approval of the principle of delegation, especially to Boroughs and Districts of 60,000 population or more, and listed the services or functions in which the principle should operate.

The policy outlined in the first White Paper was implemented, with minor changes, in the Local Government Act 1958, and Local Government Commissions were established for

England and Wales to reshape the local government map. The Act did not deal comprehensively with the subject of delegation to County Districts, but it contained a provision for schemes, requiring the Minister's approval, to be proceeded with for delegation in the personal and domiciliary health services and the welfare services, and accorded the right to Boroughs and Districts of 60,000 or over to draft and submit their own schemes to the Minister.

Thus the outcome of twenty years of discussion, consultation and controversy is that the existing pattern established in 1888 and 1894 is to be retained throughout the country except in the Greater London area (see below) and, possibly, in one or two of the conurbations. Thus none of the more radical suggestions for reform find a place in the overhaul of structure now under way. There is no doubt that the local authority associations are largely responsible for this resistance to change. The Government is generally unwilling to promote basic alterations in local government structure unless it can obtain a broad measure of agreement from a majority of those immediately concerned. Since the associations normally regard it as their business to safeguard the interests of their respective members—the various categories of local authorities—no such broad agreement on fundamental changes can be forthcoming. The insistent pressures to defend the *status quo* not only restricted the terms of reference of the Local Government Commissions but are now limiting severely the number of local changes actually being made.

THE LOCAL GOVERNMENT COMMISSIONS

The Local Government Commissions are guided in their work by a set of Regulations issued by the Government under the authority of the Local Government Act, 1958. The Regulations instruct the Commissions to establish 'effective and convenient local government' and to pay attention to the following points when remodelling areas:—

(a)   community of interest;
(b)   development and expected development;
(c)   economic and industrial characteristics;
(d)   financial resources measured in relation to financial need;

(e)   physical features, including suitable boundaries, means of communication and accessibility to administrative centres and centres of business and social life;
(f)   population—size, distribution and characterisics;
(g)   record of administration of the local authorities concerned;
(h)   size and shape of the areas of local government;
(i)   wishes of the inhabitants.

These items are not set out in order of importance: it will be noticed that the order is alphabetical. Nor are these pointers exclusive, for the Commisssions may take other matters into account if they wish so to do. A population of 100,000 is presumed to be adequate for the proper discharge of the duties of a county borough; a smaller population will be regarded as sufficient only in special circumstances.

As noted above, the Commissions were instructed to carry out their tasks within the present framework of county and county borough organisation. Thus they can propose the creation or amalgamation and demotion of county boroughs; they can suggest boundary adjustments between top-tier authorities. In the conurbations (described in the 1958 Act as the special review areas of Tyneside, West Yorkshire, South-East Lancashire, Merseyside and the West Midlands) the English Commission does have wider powers, for it can propose in these areas the establishment of a 'continuous county' in which there would be no county boroughs and in which the distribution of functions between the county and the second-tier authorities might depart from the normal pattern. Also in the special review areas the English Commission has to consider the boundaries of the district and non-county borough councils.

The Local Government Commission for England has divided the country into areas and is studying them piecemeal: the Welsh Commission dealt with its task as a whole. As a start, the Commissions hold preliminary consultations with local authorities and then issue draft proposals. Before changes can take place, there is a long road to travel. First, the local authorities concerned have a right to lodge objections and to hold a formal conference with the Commission. The Commission then submit their plans, with or without modifications, to the Ministry of Housing and Local Government. The

Minister will then invite further comment and objections from the local authorities and may arrange for a further public enquiry to be held. Ultimately the Minister must decide the issues in dispute and place the Government view before Parliament in the form of an Order which requires parliamentary approval. After all this, once any adjustments to its own boundaries have been settled, each county must review non-county boroughs, district councils and parishes: as usual, final decisions on any changes will be subject to ministerial approval.

It follows that the reorganisation of local authorities is a protracted business. Plenty of opportunity is given for public opinion to make itself felt; the force of opinion may cause a Commission to change its mind or lead the Minister to reject the final plans of a Commission. There is a tendency for each stage of decision-making to reduce the amount of change. This is well illustrated by developments in the East Midlands. Originally, the English Commission wished to amalgamate into a single administrative county the existing counties of Cambridgeshire, Isle of Ely, Huntingdonshire and the Soke of Peterborough, together with small parts of Rutland, Northamptonshire and Lincoln (Kesteven). The city of Cambridge was to become a county borough and the remainder of Rutland was to be incorporated with Leicestershire. These ideas caused a chorus of protest and criticism from local interests adversely affected; the resistance of Rutland attracted considerable national publicity. The final plan of the Commission showed major changes from their preliminary suggestions. Rutland was not to be divided but combined with Leicestershire as a whole. The Lincolnshire boundary was untouched. Most important of all, the proposed four-county amalgamation was dropped: instead the Soke of Peterborough was to join Huntingtonshire to make one new county, while the Isle of Ely would link with Cambridgeshire to make a second new county. The recommendation to make the City of Cambridge a county borough was withdrawn because without the support of the City the new county of Cambridge would be too weak to provide effective local administration. Naturally the City objected to the loss of the prospect of independence, especially as the Commission had accepted that it possessed adequate resources to become an efficient county borough. The Minister accepted the second plan with the important difference that Rutland was reprieved and is to continue as a separate county. This was, of course, a great victory for those people in Rutland who had campaigned so vigorously to retain their independence. It must give encouragement to others elsewhere who object to the Commission's ideas for their own locality.

Public opinion has also inhibited change in Wales. The problem here is that the counties, especially those in central Wales, have small populations which are scattered across a beautiful, but often infertile, countryside; in consequence, rateable values are low and the local authorities have inadequate financial resources to maintain a standard of public services comparable with that enjoyed in other areas. The Commission for Wales intended to deal with this situation by a drastic plan of county amalgamations which would have reduced the number of Welsh counties from thirteen to seven. Anglesey alone was to remain intact. Inevitably, the plan was hotly opposed in Wales. Local patriotism was incensed by the complete disregard of existing county boundaries and some of the new counties proposed were both large and inconvenient in shape. The Welsh Commission itself regarded the proposals as less that the optimum for it argued in its Report 'that an investigation of local government which is to be fully effective must go beyond a consideration of its boundaries to that of its structure, its functions and its finance'. This need is commonly stressed by students of local government and it was, of course, central to the ideas of the ill-fated Boundary Commission of 1945. It is also a principle that Ministers in the past have been reluctant to accept. However, in 1964, the Minister of Housing and Local Government announced that a fresh examination of Welsh local government would have to be made embracing both finance and functions. Meanwhile, the scheme for seven counties has been rejected, so the Welsh Commission's work has proved fruitless save for minor adjustments to county borough boundaries.

In its scheme for Tyneside the English Commission has used its power to relate areas and functions in the special review areas, whereas in West Yorkshire and the West Midlands it adhered to existing types of authorities. The Tyneside plan is for a new county authority which would embrace all of the Tyneside conurbation. Within the county would be four county districts based on four county boroughs, Newcastle-on-Tyne, Tynemouth, South Shields and Gateshead, which would be combined with adjacent lesser authorities for this purpose. The demotion of four county boroughs would be a most serious step, especially in the case of Newcastle which has a population of 270,000, but the Commission argued that only by the creation of a single authority covering the whole of Tyneside could the major planning problems of the area be solved, notably housing, the location of industry and the development of communications. The county authority would also be responsible for police, fire, ambulance and civil defence, but more personal services including education, health and welfare would remain with the four county districts which would have a wider range of functions than other second-tier authorities. Thus in Tyneside the Commission is suggesting not merely geographical changes but also a new division of responsibility between upper and lower tier authorities.

It is not surprising that the proposals of the Local Government Commissions have aroused widespread opposition, for proponents of local government reform are automatic targets for certain lines of attack. They are said to be tidy-minded and over-willing to sacrifice established institutions and loyalties for the sake of dull uniformity. Certainly reformers commonly fail to appreciate the extent and the value of local patriotism. Councillors who have given much service to a local authority cannot be expected to welcome its projected demise and they resent any implication that their council has been unable to carry out its duties with full efficiency. Local government officers, especially chief officials, fear for the effect of change on their personal status. It is commonly argued without any evidence that proposed alterations will have an adverse effect on the level of the rate poundage. Behind these forces of local opinion stand the national pressure groups, the associations of local authorities, ready to do what they can to safeguard the interests of their members.

Against all this must be set the propositions that the present structure of local government is insupportable in theory and constantly works ill in practice. Ever since 1945 it has been Government policy that local government needs reform. There must, of course, be a variety of views about the advantages of any specific proposals: there will always be a mass of special pleading designed to show why any individual local authority should be an exception to any general principle of area revision.

The ultimate decisions resting with the Minister of Housing and Local Government are essentially complex and awkward. To date, the most striking decision has been the reprieve of Rutland. If a county council serving a mere 25,000 people is to continue, what justification can there be for amalgamating any other counties? Indeed, since every county borough has more inhabitants than Rutland, why should any county borough be demoted? Certainly, population is not the sole yardstick by which to measure whether an authority can provide efficient services; but population statistics do provide a simple, uncomplicated test which is persuasive to the public mind. It is easy, after Rutland, to argue that all ministerial decisions about the future of local government lack courage and ignore the crying need to make changes essential to meet the requirements of our time. Such a view, however, is untenable. In contrast to Rutland, there is London, where a major upheaval in local administration has been carried through.

LONDON GOVERNMENT

The task of reforming local government in the London area was unique in magnitude. Over eight million people, roughly a sixth of the population of England and Wales, are clustered together in the Greater London conurbation. In 1957 the Government decided that the problem was so vast as to need separate treatment; a Royal Commission was appointed to study the complexities of the metropolitan area which was therefore excluded from the purview of the Local Government Commission for England. The central difficulty was the absence of any local authority which embraced the whole of the Greater London area. The London County Council inherited its boundary from the Metropolitan Board of Works which was established in 1855; while it represents the geographical realities of a century ago, this boundary has no relevance to the facts of the present day. London spilled over into large sections of Kent, Surrey, Hertford, Essex and the whole of Middlesex. Little more than a third of the population of Greater London lived within the L.C.C. area, and the L.C.C.

population of 3,200,000 was still declining slowly. There were also three county boroughs in Greater London, Croydon, East Ham and West Ham, so it followed that nine top-tier authorities in the London area were each responsible for broad issues of planning policy. No single local authority could have a synoptic view of the issues connected with the re-development and zoning of Greater London, the movement of population and the construction of main traffic arteries. In the counties surrounding the L.C.C. there were no fewer than fourteen county districts with more than 100,000 inhabitants. These authorities, had they been situated elsewhere, would have had an automatic claim to county borough status. As it was, the larger county districts in suburban London commonly shared in county functions through a system of delegation by the county councils. Delegation is a somewhat cumbrous arrangement which runs smoothly only if there is full co-operation between the parties thereto. In many cases it has worked well: elsewhere, notably in Middlesex, it did not. Inside the L.C.C. area were the City of London and the 28 Metropolitan Boroughs created in 1899, which were also of uneven size,—Wandsworth had 338,000 inhabitants and Holborn had 21,000. L.C.C. delegation to the Metropolitan Boroughs was negligible.

This in brief outline was the situation facing the Royal Commission. Its Report, Cmnd. 1164 of 1960, unanimously urged drastic changes. The Commission was of opinion that a Council for Greater London should be established to be responsible for overall planning, main roads, fire and ambulance services. It would also share responsibility for education, housing, planning applications and certain other services with a new type of second-tier authority—Greater London Boroughs. These Greater London Boroughs would have the status and constitution of municipal boroughs except that the City of London would be permitted to retain its present institutions. The Commission's scheme envisaged 52 of these Boroughs with populations between 100,000 and 250,000,—except, again, for the City of London: they would be responsible for health and welfare services, child care, local roads and libraries, in addition to the duties shared with the Council for Greater London. Reorganization on this scale involved the disappearance of the L.C.C., Middlesex and three county boroughs, substantial loss of territory and rateable value by four county councils, and extensive amalgamations of county districts and metropolitan boroughs. It is thus not surprising that this Report also aroused substantial opposition.

In this instance, however, the Government were not deflected by local hostility. They accepted the broad lines of the Royal Commission's Report and the London Government Act, 1963, now provides an opportunity for the co-ordinated planning of the whole metropolitan area. There were some modifications to the Commission's proposals. The number of London Boroughs was reduced from 52 to 32. There were two reasons for this change: first, some fringe areas were excluded from the London area altogether and remain in Surrey and Essex, and second, and far more important, the minimum population of London Boroughs was doubled. This rise to 200,000 was due partly to the further decision that London Boroughs shall have full powers over education—save in the former L.C.C. territory where a committee of the Greater London Council, representing the area concerned, has this responsibility.

The challenge facing the new Greater London Council is formidable and exciting. Its size and scope dwarf all other of our local authorities. There is now the chance to provide cohesive direction to the development of the national capital and its environs. No doubt, some time must pass before a fair assessment can be made of the achievements of the G.L.C. But if it reaches a high level of success, if it demonstrates the effectiveness of action on a regional scale, then students and critics of local government will soon urge the need for larger units of local administration in other parts of our land.

CHAPTER X

Problems of Today and Tomorrow

FUNCTIONS

AFTER MORE THAN a century of growth and expansion, the responsibilities of English Local Authorities attained their apogee in 1939; and, as they then stood, were far and away the heaviest and widest undertaken by any similar bodies throughout the world. The series of nationalization measures inaugurated in 1945 brought the first serious check that the system had suffered. They involved the transfer of municipal hospitals, gas undertakings, and electricity undertakings to other agencies.

Proposals for the nationalization of water supply did not materialize. Nevertheless the curtailment has been substantial so far as it has already gone. It would be a gross exaggeration to say that local government is now only a shadow of its former self: its scope is still wider than in most other countries; but it has manifestly lost its old pre-eminent lead.

These recent events have brought into the political forum a question which would have been thought academic earlier in this century: what ought the scope of local government to be? It is one that the local government world—and many outside it—now ask with some disquiet. This disquiet is prompted not merely by the loss of functions already sustained but by the fear that other functions may go the same way.

We can eliminate at once any bearing the question has, in the form in which it is asked, upon party controversy as to the scope of government in general. When asked, as it can be, and in fact is, without party colouring, it is directed to the choice of agency for whatever functions go to make up the sphere of government and public administration as national policy determines it. Even so it is a question so wide and complex that only the broad considerations which enter into it can be adduced here.

These fall broadly into two categories: considerations of

political principle, and considerations of administrative necessity, efficiency, and convenience. They do not provide us with
a formula, deciding the general content of local government,
or the right allocation of particular sectors of public administration. Each case has to be looked at in the light of both considerations, and a decision made on a balance of them.

Those who champion local government agency on grounds
of political principle will be unrealistic and unwise if they fail
to recognize that a situation has been reached in which administrative considerations enter more fully into the question today
than they did in the earlier phases of local government. It is
manifest indeed that administrative considerations have been
behind many of the recent changes which have come over local
government—the upgrowth of certain forms of central control,
as well as recent losses of function. And one reason for this is
the simple one that other agencies exist!—whereas for a long
time, during which local government had got under very considerable way, they did *not* exist—or at any rate not in their
present highly developed forms. The highly competent Civil
Service of today was largely a product of the latter part of the
nineteenth century; and even in the early part of the present
century the organizational resources of government departments were rudimentary. Nor had political, social, and
economic developments yet given birth to the conception of
the public corporation, designed to act in the economic or administrative sphere with the scope and organizational framework of the large industrial entrepreneur. In this situation function after function—including many which reflected national
as well as local needs—fell to local government without any
serious call for the consideration of alternative agency.

A further factor to be taken into account—revealing itself
in much recent history of local government services—is that
services which may start on the footing of local 'markets' or
jurisdictions may encounter new conditions which impress
them with some of the features of national services, and call
for some measure of central organization, direction, and lay-
out of plant and equipment, e.g. electricity supply. Administrative requirements may often be satisfied by some process of
fitting local executive control into a national plan; but often
the public corporation or government department has been
deemed to be the optimum unit of organisation.

And finally, this or the other local service may be affected by population changes, knitting local communities together and having their impact upon local government structure. Arguments may be raised for some more elastic and specialized structure for that particular service. Its specific requirements may stand out in high relief. The virtues of its association with other services under one local control may lie more in the background, and go unnoticed or unappreciated.

It is clear that local government has no longer an extensive claim to conduct services on grounds of administrative necessity. It can still raise many claims of its own on grounds of administrative efficiency and convenience for the conduct of services local in character, or requiring or allowing of a local basis or organization; and everything we have said as to the virtues of the municipal machine is in point here. Through the pre-existent scope of local government itself, new conditions have tended to emphasize the national aspect of public services. The future may emphasize the requirements and the virtues of their local aspects.

Support for local government on grounds of political principle springs from a persistent strain in English political thinking which conceives of representative government itself as calling for distribution over two planes, local as well as central. In the heyday of individualist doctrine this view may largely have rested upon the sentiment that government of any kind being a necessary evil, local government is a less evil than central. As collectivist tendencies grew, it was reinforced by the feeling that if the scope of government must expand, a substantial content for local government could provide a desirable check upon the power of the central executive and its agents; and underneath this feeling no doubt lay the general idea of the virtues of a separation and balance of powers in the constitutional sphere.

In its essentials this line of thought and feeling is still cogent in the conditions of today. It has in fact been strengthened by modern illustrations of what can happen to states democratic in form but in which democracy has rested on little else than a mass vote cast periodically upon the national plane. As more and more people are coming to realize, democracy must be multiform, and strike its roots in social groupings and communities of many kinds, and not merely that grouping we call the State, artificial as it can often be. In the local communities with which it is concerned, local government brings together men and women of very different creed, outlook, and station in life for practical co-operation in accepted tasks and interests; and English local government history itself can illustrate all that this means in building up a democracy at once progressive, resilient, and stable.

The outstanding factor which calls for emphasis is the opportunity that local government presents for practical education in political and social responsibility. No other single agency of government presents it on so wide a front, or so continuously. No other agency draws the ordinary citizen into the actual processes of government as local government does. No form of political education can be better than this, and no democratic state can ultimately dispense with it. Political capacity can only be developed by the exercise of active political responsibility.

These considerations point to one broad rubric: local (representative) government should be accorded a first preference in our mental approach to the choice of agency in all cases where services can be run, or functions exercised, on the basis of local jurisdictions or 'markets'. We may at times have to recognize the predominance of national characteristics in some service or function, and a necessity for central direction; but even services with conspicuous traits of this kind should be examined to see what place can be afforded for local administration through local representative government. This outlook still does not furnish us with a formula: it furnishes us with an approach; but an approach which many factors combine to show as the right one.

CENTRAL—LOCAL RELATIONSHIPS

Whatever the content of local government activity is to be, it now seems unlikely that the English practice of specific Parliamentary authorization for it will seriously be called into question. In some quarters it used to be suggested that the *ultra vires* rule should be reversed; and that Local Authorities, instead of being empowered to do only what Parliament expressly sanctions, should be empowered to do anything except that which Parliament expressly prohibits. So radical a change is not likely to be achieved without a much greater shift

L

of opinion towards collectivism than any which has so far expressed itself electorally. The Labour Party when in opposition repeatedly presented a Local Authorities Enabling Bill to give effect to such a change in principle; but it did not pursue this line of policy when in office, and indeed the recent and present national situation is on many scores different from that which existed in the days when the Labour Party presented its measure.

Some countries which operate the alternative principle, e.g. Germany in pre-Nazi days, have claimed that their systems have in consequence a greater measure of autonomy than ours; but financial and central controls are operative as a set off which have prevented the local government of these countries from attaining any wider scope than in England.

The only major question which arises in regard to the judicial control over Local Authorities is that of the right kind of tribunal for the hearing of appeals from administrative decisions of the Local Authorities on matters, mostly within the sphere of the protective and regulative services, in which the task of the Local Authority is quasi-judicial. Legislative practice as a whole is not very consistent in the allocation of appellate jurisdiction of this kind. Sometimes the ordinary Courts, such as the Justices Court and the Court of Quarter Sessions, are given jurisdiction, sometimes the Ministries, and sometimes special tribunals. Local Authorities have no such fears about ousting the ordinary Courts from jurisdiction of this kind as agitate the constitutional lawyers. Many local authorities—perhaps most—prefer appellate jurisdiction of this kind to be vested in the Ministries or special tribunals, rather than in the ordinary Courts; at any rate, Courts of the kind which have jurisdiction in such matters. If they are to be rallied in support of Dicey's doctrines on this topic, they will have to be convinced that Courts of Petty Sessions and Quarter Sessions are as competent as the Ministries or the special tribunals in work of this kind, and as consistent and fair.

We pass now to some observations on the topic of central administrative controls. Beyond doubt the extent to which these have expanded and become more detailed and continuous in character has given rise to much disquiet. The problem of reducing and limiting them to what reasonable people in the worlds of both central and local government might agree to be their necessary content—there are many who would say that this should be a necessary minimum—would be much simpler than it really is if the main cause of their proliferation had been a calculated design on the part of the Government departments to attract more and more powers to the centre. There are some in the local government world who have averred that this is so: but while some allowance is to be made for what is called 'empire building' in every human institution this explanation of the situation is not one that can be seriously accepted, and to accept it as the main factor which has led to the present situation would only obscure the problem and render it less likely of solution.

For the most part, controls have sprung up or expanded through the pressure of national conditions, national policies, and, indeed, the public sentiment which national policies have reflected, upon the tasks the local authorities fulfil or the services they conduct. Nor, if we could review in detail all the particular matters over which the controls operate in one form or another, and what is aimed at in each case, would we find any serious proportion of instances in which the control is groundless. Nearly always we should discover some cogent reason, founded upon the benefit of the public, the safeguarding of its interests or its purse, or the protection of individual rights.

In advising on new legislation, especially on measures of a new kind, or those in which the State as well as the municipal purse is involved, the Government departments have no doubt felt it their duty, quite rightly, to concern themselves with all levels of public control, central as well as local; but it has nevertheless often appeared that they themselves have viewed with considerable distaste the extent to which they have felt obliged or been compelled by national policy, to resort to the more meticulous types of control. Indeed, the traditional attitude of the older departments has been to avoid anything which brought them too much into the executive sphere while retaining firm hold on the broader and more ultimate types of administrative control. Perhaps the most serious criticism is that the central administrative machine has not been able to visualize the total impact of all the controls exercised by all the departments, and the impact in terms of delay, administrative cost, and manpower, at both the central and local levels.

There are, and will no doubt continue to be, aspects in the central-local relationship—some general, others arising in the conduct of particular services—which justify certain types of central administrative control in principle and in aim.

Services which though locally administered are provided in response to national and not merely local needs must conform to some kind of national plan; and in complex and often rapidly changing conditions, central administrative control may often be the only effective agency to fit the localized activity into the national plan. Even before nationalization, municipal (as well as company) electricity undertakings had to submit to the jurisdiction of the Electricity Commissioners in technical matters, the function of generation had been concentrated with some undertakers and removed from others, and the current produced was handled on the wholesale side by the central Electricity Board through its network of main transmission, i.e. 'the grid'. Municipal transport undertakings came, and still come, under the jurisdiction of Traffic Commissioners in some aspects of fares and routes. In these two instances services whose original characteristics were almost purely local developed regional or national characteristics through technical or demographic change. In others which come within the same general category, as for example education, the service may have possessed its national characteristics from the outset, and the real impetus to central controls has been the public expectation of standards or uniformities in the service as a whole, irrespective of the area of administration. On the considerations mentioned already in the discussion of functions, it is surely better for local government to retain such services wherever possible, and to submit to all essential central control of them, rather than to lose them.

Nor is any elaborate analysis necessary to recognize the logic of central controls which stem from the financial aid given to local government by the state.

The questions which remain when the legitimate ground of central control is recognized are as to method and measure. Need the controls be as detailed and meticulous in a system so mature as our own? If they must sometimes be applied in fairly specific forms originally, need these forms go on by rote when first objectives are realized? Above all, has a stage not now been reached when the value of the controls needs to be reassessed in the light not only of their general impact on the principles of local self-government but of their own heavy cost in terms of manpower at both levels? Some simplifications of central control were achieved after the 1950 Report of the Local Government Manpower Committee, but this is essentially a problem which calls for periodic re-examination.

The independence of local authorities has been deeply undermined by their reliance on financial help from the central government. Inevitably, 'he who pays the piper calls the tune'. Local authorities have had to seek increased central aid because it has been so difficult politically to augment their income from rates sufficiently to keep pace with rising costs and growing responsibilities. It is undisputed that local rates are a most unsatisfactory form of taxation for there is no certain correlation, as there is with income-tax, between the amount an individual has to pay and his capacity to pay. A lodger pays no rates at all, at least directly. A man with a large family needs a large house; because of his family he will have to pay more in rates whereas on the principles of equity, as applied in income-tax law, his family should reduce tax liability and not increase it. Revaluation of property has lagged far behind changes in price levels and property values. There has been also great psychological objection to levying rates above 20/- in the pound. Thus the resistance to paying higher rates, aggravated by the unfairness of the system, has effectively reduced the taxing capacity of local councils, and has led to incessant demands for more state subsidies. It is widely argued that education—easily the most expensive local government service—is a national service and, as such, should be financed entirely by the national Exchequer. Yet, if it were, how far would it continue to be a local government service if local education authorities had no financial responsibility save to the Minister of Education?

Local government would be immensely strengthened if it could acquire additional taxing power. Various new types of local tax have been suggested,—a local income tax, taxation of site values and motor taxation which local authorities now collect but pass on to the national government. So far none of these suggestions have found favour. The objections to them are partly political, partly administrative, and the issues are too involved and technical to be fully considered here. But if the local rate is not replaced or supplemented as the means of local taxation, it is difficult to see how to stop the further erosion of the effective independence of our local councils.

DISTRICT AUDIT

The topic of Government audit deserves some special notice, for it involves issues on which there has been at times much strong feeling in the world of local government. Few Local Government Officers—and it is the officers who are best able to judge—would deny that Government audit, or 'District audit' as it is called, is efficient—at any rate in recent decades. It is certainly not inferior to professional audit as an audit of accounts. Indeed as the Government Auditors work in a specialist field and have developed their own expertise, there is reason to believe that it is more efficient, taken over the whole field. It is, as we have seen, also concerned with the legality of expenditure, and the auditor is armed with powers not available to professional auditors. The statutory direction given to a Government auditor to disallow all expenditure 'contrary to law' and to surcharge it upon those he considers responsible for it—i.e. make them liable to pay it personally—could hardly give him a more drastic jurisdiction.

As a result, Government audit is a more rigorous process for the Local Authority and its officers than professional audit. For this very reason few public-spirited councillors and officers, desirous of accepting every test of healthy administration, would desire anything else than Government audit, were it not for what they regard as the unwarrantable powers vested in the auditor. That the Government auditor should be able to say that expenditure is *ultra vires*, or illegal in character, and have powers of surcharge, is not generally contested; but as we have seen, the expenditure is 'contrary to law' if it is unreasonably excessive. This situation is the result of a general rule of common law that an administrative body such as a Local Authority must exercise any discretion given to it by statute 'reasonably'. If, therefore, it spends at an 'unreasonable' level, its expenditure is 'contrary to law' within the meaning of that phrase in the statutory provisions relating to the auditor's functions; and as the Local Government Act directs the Government auditor to disallow expenditure 'contrary to law' he is forced to disallow any expenditure which is 'unreasonable', and put into the position of having to form his own view as to whether expenditure is reasonable or not.

This position endows the auditor with a wide power—nay indeed, a duty—to canvass questions of policy involved in the level of expenditure on some item or object, to intervene, and to surcharge, as guided solely by his own judgment; for there are many matters in which views may vary very considerably as to what is reasonable and what is unreasonable. It is surely wrong that in a sphere in which the political and constitutional sense of the nation has on the whole left the exercise of discretion to an elected body, language used in an Act passed to provide for audits (possibly without appreciation of the content imported into it by a general rule of law) should empower an individual official to substitute his judgment for the elected Council's—for that is what in fact the power amounts to. The auditors are appointed by the Minister and are under his jurisdiction from a staffing and establishment point of view, but the Ministry aver that they do not control him in the exercise of his functions, i.e. he exercises the functions, duties, and powers given to him by the statute independently and in his own right. There are rights of appeal on surcharge to the High Court, or, in respect of a sum less than £500, either the High Court or the Minister. While this right of appeal is no doubt a considerable safeguard, it may be doubted whether even the powers of a Judge or a Minister to say what is reasonable or not, on a question involving policy for which an elected Council is politically responsible to the electorate, are given any more properly to them than the auditor's powers in this respect are given to him. But it is right to say that on the whole the Judges have themselves been studiously anxious not to trespass into the sphere of Local Authority discretion, and have seldom taken an unreasonable view of what is 'unreasonable', in appeals against the auditors' decisions.

It is only fair to say, too, that the Minister is given a power to dispense from disallowance and surcharge by a proviso in the relevant statutory provisions that 'no expenses paid by an authority shall be disallowed by the auditor if they have been sanctioned by the Minister'. Ministerial sanction cannot, however, legalise illegal expenditure. It removes it from the jurisdiction of the auditor, but cannot remove a ratepayer's right of resort to the Courts. Moreover, the Minister regards his dispensing powers as exercisable only within limits. The guide used to be the following pronouncement of the old Local Government Board:

> 'The power of sanction is intended to be used in those cases where expenditure is incurred bona fide but in ignorance of the strict letter of the law, or inadvertently without the observance of the requisite formalities, or under such circumstances as make it fair and equitable that the expenditure should not be disallowed by the audit. We do not regard the Act as intended to supply the want of legislative or other authority for particular expenditure or classes of expenditure, and as justifying us in giving prospective sanction to recurring expenditure.'

The Minister's dispensing power is no longer needed to cover minor expenditure of dubious legality for the Local Government (Financial Provisions) Act, 1963, allows a local authority to incur expenditure up to the amount of a penny rate for any purpose which in its opinion would benefit the area, provided that such activity is not subject to other statutory provision. Thus local councils have new freedom on items of small-scale expenditure. It will be interesting to observe how far this new power is utilised. If it is ignored, the implication would seem to be that the *ultra vires* doctrine has not in the past been a true barrier to local initiative, but rather a convenient excuse for inaction.

Today the District Auditor seems much less of an ogre than he did thirty years ago. He more rarely raises issues about the reasonableness of expenditure. Perhaps there is less need for him to do so. Local authorities are now conditioned to accept central directions through a wide range of administrative controls, and so are more unlikely to engage in unorthodox spending. Political conflicts over local government services are not so acute as in the nineteen-twenties: partly this is because public assistance has become a matter for national administration. Some people in a position to judge also believe that the Auditor is now more elastic in his approach to *ultra vires* issues. Also, instead of imposing a surcharge, he may give a private warning that certain expenditure is questionable and should not be repeated.

Even so, the basic objection to the system remains—that the views of elected representatives on the desirability of expenditure can be over-borne by a civil servant. This objection is not removed by the existence of the Ministerial dispensing power or the Minister's power to remit a surcharge. If, as the result of error of judgement, as distinct from wilful disregard of clear statutory direction, or corrupt intent, Councillors have incurred 'unreasonable' expenditure, it is little comfort for them to be told they can appeal, or that even if found guilty the sentence may not be carried out. Some County Boroughs, and most of the older Boroughs, none of which can be compelled to submit to District audit, except of grant-aided services, will have nothing to do with it, obviously because they will not suffer to be told by an auditor what expenditure is reasonable and what is not, or to expose themselves to the hazard of judging in advance what the state of the auditor's mind is on questions of pubic policy. Such a situation is regrettable, because they could not fail to profit from the skilled audit of accountancy, and of legality in the more ordinary sense of the term, which Government audit can provide.

DEFECTS IN LOCAL ADMINISTRATION

The system of local administration in England is prone to three defects: first, an undue absorption of the elected personnel in administrative detail, to the neglect of major functions in the spheres of policy and planning; secondly, the difficuty of co-ordinating committees and departments; and thirdly, the failure to make any constitutional provision for a centre of initiative and drive. All three weaknesses accrue through the establishment of one body, and that an elected Council, to be responsible for matters of administration as well as matters of policy.

Much can be done to prevent or counteract these weaknesses by making that creative use of officers which we referred to in Chapter VI. Thus, in Councils where both elected and official personnel possess the right administrative sense, administrative detail is left to the officers, and the elected representatives concentrate on their major functions of policy. Yet it is never possible to draw the line rigidly between questions of policy and questions of administration. An intermediate sphere exists in which the councillors and officers must collaborate, the possibility of such a collaboration being one of those features of the municipal system which we have claimed as a virtue. Where good administrative sense is lacking, on either side, there is no safeguard against an undue interference by elected personnel with the administrative process, and nothing to secure a proper allocation of time and attention to larger matters of policy. Much can be done by properly framed Standing Orders, and by committees such as the Finance Committee, to secure the co-ordination of committee work; and we have already discussed the ways in which it is possible for the chief administrative officer to secure co-ordination of departments. It is possible, too, for the chief officers, and in particular the Clerk, to assume a large measure of initiative in putting forward measures of policy, and long-term plans, to the several committees, and to mark out broad roads of civil ambition for the Council as a whole.

The Committee system itself is an attempt to eliminate some of the defects referred to. Its fuller development, as described in Chapter VII, besides effecting a useful division of executive work which gives the Council the opportunity to concentrate on the larger issues, establishes financial co-ordination, through the agency of the Finance Committee, which must to some extent enable the Council to co-ordinate policy as well. Much good can be done at times by setting up a Future Policy Committee to make out the broader objects of Council policy which concern the work of all committees. Where a highly developed committee organization is in existence, and where a chief administrative officer functions in the way described in Chapter VIII, the weaknesses in the system may well be eradicated. We have described them as defects to which the system is prone, not as defects it cannot escape.

The author's impression is that in most cases measures of the kind mentioned are sufficient, or would be sufficient if applied, to eliminate any idea of a radical change of system. Yet it is possible that in the largest Authorities measures of the kind referred to in Chapters VII and VIII have gone to the utmost possible limit, and that the tasks arising in the post-war world will make existing machinery creak and groan. Take, for example, the first problem. It is already said that we lose in some measure the typical virtue of the English system in the large county Authorities where there is a large delegation of powers to committees, and where meetings of these are so infrequent and the areas so scattered as to preclude any effective oversight of administration. The situation which could arise in places of this kind is a complete dilemma between an undue concentration upon administration and a complete elimination of elected personnel from any effective oversight of it. Again, the range of work may be so vast in the largest of our cities that control and co-ordination should be a continuous process, watchful over policy as a whole and over the whole of the executive work of applying it, and that neither the committees nor the chief administrative officer may have time to do it adequately, the committees because they are composed of only part-time personnel, the chief administrative officer because as Clerk to the Authority he has himself executive responsibilities of the most extensive character. Finally, in the very large Authorities it may be doubted whether any single man such as a Clerk can assume an initiative which extends to every sphere of policy; unless, at any rate, he is relieved of his own executive responsibilities as secretary and legal officer.

In the British national constitution, and in local government abroad, the conditions analysed above have been met by the establishment of a separate executive organ, and it is in this direction that local government in Britain may have to move if problems of the kind referred to become more acute, or get beyond the reach of measures of the kind referred to in Chapters VII and VIII, as in the largest places they might do.

The earliest modern prototype of a municipal régime based on this system was the Burgomaster system of pre-Nazi Germany, in which the Burgomaster was the head of the Executive, with powers of his own in that sphere, and also had the responsibility of preparing and putting forward the budget, and initiating measures of policy for the elected Council's approval. The subsequent history of Germany may render the model a distasteful one to British sentiment, as an early example of the German liking for authoritarian organization. The German Burgomaster was also a State officer, an arrangement not inherent in the model itself.

In its local aspect, the same model prevails in the Scandinavian countries as well as in Holland and Belgium. There is a

similar separation of powers between the elected Council and
its Executive. In some instances the Executive is a small group
of which the Burgomaster is chief with some special powers of
his own, e.g. the Burgomaster and Vethoulders of the Dutch
towns, or the Magistraat in some Scandinavian countries.

These arrangements cannot be dismissed as undemocratic,
though they may fall behind the English committee system in
the opportunity they afford for the rank and file of the elected
personnel to be educated by a wider participation in the whole
process of local government and administration.

It is in democratic America that the newest model of municipal government, namely the Council-and-Manager model,
replacing in many towns the old Mayor-and-Council, or the
temporary Commissioner system, has returned to the Burgomaster model—for the two systems are different only in name.
There is an elected Council entrusted with the general control
of policy and the purse-strings, but a qualified individual
Executive, called the City Manager, is appointed, with powers
of his own. He occupies a position similar to that of a Managing
Director in the business world, is the head of 'the administration', with complete powers in the executive sphere; prepares
the budget for the Council's approval, and has the constitutional duty of advising, formulating, and putting forward
measures of policy over the whole range of municipal activity.
This system is working successfully and efficiently in America,
and just before 1940 was carried into the counties and the
smaller county towns of the Irish Free State, after operating in
the cities there for some years previously. The Free State
County Management Act of 1939 embodies in its most highly
developed and safeguarded form the system thus introduced
into the Irish Free State. The Council retains complete power in
the sphere of policy, all functions of policy being specified in a
schedule to the Act. The residue of the Local Authority's legal
powers comprises the administrative scope of the Manager, and
the exercise of these powers is left entirely to him, subject to
budgetary limitations. The Manager can put forward advice on
policy and he prepares the budget for the Council's approval.
Just as Parliament can dismiss the Executive, so the Council
can dismiss the Manager, but only with central consent.

It will be seen that in essence all the foregoing systems are
on the lines of the British Cabinet system in the national

sphere. How could such a system be introduced into British local government? If it comes at all, it is not unlikely in England to come by adaptation of the existing model; and it is thus much more likely to take the Scandinavian form of an executive group rather than a single City Manager. It may come by giving a constitutional cachet to the chairmen of committees as a group. Already, in the larger places, the chairmen are coming to function as an informal executive group giving day-to-day decisions; and we have seen the extent to which, as a team, they comprise the whole of, or the leading element in, committees such as the Finance, Staffs, and Works Committees, discharging functions of a kind left to the separate executive in other systems. Short of constitutional recognition and regulation there may be some danger of informal agencies of this kind degenerating into juntas, political or personal.

It may well be that any constitutional recognition of an executive in English local government would favour an executive group, representative of, and to some degree dependent on, and perhaps chosen out of, the elected personnel, as in the case of a British Ministry or Cabinet. This would be more in keeping with British sentiment; but it is precisely this intermediate type of personnel that might prove the most difficult to introduce. They would give continuous and probably whole-time service but would be neither appointed officials nor lay representatives. If the executive are to be whole-time they will need to be paid. If they are adequately paid, for real responsibility and administrative ability, they will become indistinguishable from the officers; though perhaps not as efficient, because they will have no security of tenure and will lack the skill and experience of men who have made this work a career. On the other hand, if they are paid but a pittance they will tend to be dominated, either by the retired classes, or by persons of inadequate ability and experience.

In the larger authorities, leading councillors and aldermen, including the chairmen of major committees, already devote a great deal of time each week to public service. Clearly, only a limited section of the community are in a position to undertake these duties for financial reasons. Thus councils are composed of retired persons, wealthy persons, housewives, the self-employed and a few people fortunate enough to have employers willing to release them for their local government work. This must limit the availability of potential councillors and the loss-of-time allowance introduced in 1948 has done little to change the situation. From this it is tempting to argue that the councillors on the larger authorities, perhaps reduced in number, should *all* be paid. Is this not the only way to try and ensure that our elected representatives constitute a fair cross-section of age groups and income groups? But the objections are great. First, as was noted above, there is the question of how much should be paid, and the implications of that decision. Then is there any evidence that payment would improve the quality of councillors? Would people be attracted to local government for the wrong reason i.e. personal gain? Finally, it must be recognised that payment would give a new type of patronage to local political parties, since the nomination to contest a 'safe' seat would be tantamount to the award of money from public funds.

On this rather speculative theme this book must close. This concluding chapter has but sketched the topics it has dealt with, and reads more like an index to local government controversy than a contribution to it. Nevertheless, taken with what has gone before, it may have cleared the way to the fuller understanding which must come from further reading, experience, and observation; and it will have accomplished something if, as the author hopes, it has disengaged and clarified the crucial issues in the local Government problems of today and tomorrow.

APPENDIX A

POWERS AND DUTIES OF LOCAL AUTHORITIES

The following lists show the distribution between the several classes of local authority of local government services and functions in alphabetical order. They are subject to some local variations, *e.g.* Local Act Powers; some powers are mandatory and others permissive. As between councils of the same class, there are some differences in the powers and duties, dependant on the population of the district or the extent to which powers have been delegated by the County Council or conferred by the Minister of Housing and Local Government or exercised by joint boards or joint committees constituted from local authorities.

Powers and Duties of Local Authorities	County Councils	County Borough Councils	Non-County Borough Councils	Urban District Councils	Rural District Councils	Parish Councils (Rural)	Greater London Council	London Borough Councils
Abattoirs — provision and maintenance	—	Yes	Yes	Yes	Yes	—	—	Yes
Access to the Countryside	Yes	Yes	(Yes)	(Yes)	(Yes)	—	—	Yes
(where delegated)								
Administration of Justice	Yes	Yes	Some	—	—	—	Yes	—
Aerodromes, Provision of.	Yes	Yes	Yes	Yes	Yes	—	Yes	Yes
Aged and Infirm, accommodation and welfare	Yes	Yes	—	—	—	—	—	Yes
Agricultural Education	Yes	Yes	—	—	—	—	Yes	Yes
Allotments and Smallholdings	Yes	Yes	Allotments only	Allotments only	Allotments only	Allotments only	Inner London Smallholdings only	Outer London Allotments only
Alteration of areas of county districts	Yes	—	—	—	—	—	—	—
Ambulances	Yes	Yes	—	—	—	—	Yes	—

POWERS AND DUTIES OF LOCAL AUTHORITIES (*contd.*)

Powers and Duties of Local Authorities	County Councils	County Borough Councils	Non-County Borough Councils	Urban District Councils	Rural District Councils	Parish Councils (Rural)	Greater London Council	London Borough Councils
Approved Schools	Yes	Yes	—	—	—	—	Yes	—
Art Galleries — construction and supervision	Yes	Yes	Yes	Yes	Yes	Yes	Yes	Yes
Baths, swimming baths, washhouses and laundries	—	Yes	Yes	Yes	Yes	Yes	—	Yes
Betting and Gaming Act, 1960. (Permits for provision of Amusements with prizes)	—	Yes	Yes	Yes	Yes	—	—	Yes
Births, deaths and marriages registration	Yes	Yes	Yes	Yes	Yes	—	—	Yes
Blind, deaf, dumb and crippled — welfare	Yes	Yes	—	—	—	—	—	Yes
Bridges — construction and maintenance	Yes	Yes	—	—	—	—	Yes	Yes
Bridges — lighting	—	Yes	Yes	Yes	Yes	—	Yes	Yes
Building control	—	Yes	Yes	Yes	Yes	—	Yes	Yes
Building preservation	Yes	Yes	Yes	Yes	Yes	—	Inner London Yes	Outer London Yes
Burial grounds, cemeteries, crematoria and mortuaries	Crematoria only	Yes	Yes	Yes	Yes (except burial grounds)	Burial grounds and mortuaries only	—	Yes
Byelaws, various	Yes	Yes	Yes	Yes	Yes	Yes	Yes	Yes
Canal boats — registration and inspection	—	Yes	Yes	Yes	Yes	—	—	Yes
Caravans, site licences	—	Yes	Yes	Yes	Yes	—	—	—

Function							
Caravans, provision of sites	Yes	Yes	Yes	Yes	Yes	Yes	Yes
Cattle grids	Yes	Yes	Yes	Yes	Yes	Yes	Yes
Celluloid — storage control	—	Yes	Yes	Yes	Yes	—	Yes
Charities Act, 1960 (various powers)	Yes	Yes	Yes	Yes	Yes	Yes	Yes
Children — adoption, boarding out, control of employment, protection	Yes	Yes	—	—	Yes	—	Yes
Civic Restaurants	—	Yes	Yes	Yes	Yes	—	Yes
Civil Defence	Yes	Yes	Yes	Yes	Yes	Yes	Yes
Clean Air Act — Smoke Abatement	—	Yes (minor responsibilities & powers)	Yes	Yes	—	—	Yes
Clocks	Yes	Yes	Yes	Yes	Yes	Yes	Yes
Coast Protection	—	Yes	Yes	Yes	Yes	—	—
Common Lodging Houses	—	Yes	Yes	Yes	Yes	—	Yes
Commons	Yes	Yes	Yes	Yes	Yes	Yes	Yes
Community Centres	Yes	Yes	Yes	Yes	Yes	—	Yes
Consumer Protection Act, 1961	Yes	Yes	Yes	Yes	Yes	Yes	Yes
Coroners	Yes	Yes	—	—	—	Yes	—
Day Nurseries	Yes	Yes	—	—	—	—	Yes
Diseases of animals, sterilisation of waste food, foot and mouth disease	Yes	Yes	—	—	—	—	Yes
Elections	Yes	Yes	Yes	Yes	Yes	Yes	Yes
Education, including school medical service, school meals, road patrols	Yes	Yes	(Yes) where delegated or conferred under various arrangements	(Yes)	(Yes)	Yes — Inner London	Yes — Outer London
Entertainment — licensing of theatres, cinemas, race courses, music and dancing establishments, boxing and wrestling arenas	Yes	Yes	—	—	—	Yes	—
Entertainment — provision of	—	Yes	Yes	Yes	Yes	Yes	Yes

POWERS AND DUTIES OF LOCAL AUTHORITIES (contd.)

Powers and Duties of Local Authorities	County Councils	County Borough Councils	Non-County Borough Councils	Urban District Councils	Rural District Councils	Parish Councils (Rural)	Greater London Council	London Borough Councils
Explosives and fireworks	Yes	Yes	Yes	Yes	Yes	—	—	Yes
Factories — health and sanitary conditions	—	Yes	Yes	Yes	Yes	—	—	Yes
Fertilisers and feeding-stuffs — analysis	Yes	Yes	—	—	—	—	—	Yes
Fireguards inspection	—	Yes	Yes	Yes	Yes	—	—	Yes
Fire services	Yes	Yes	—	—	—	—	Yes	—
Food and Drugs — inspection, sampling and analysis	Yes	Yes	Yes	Yes	Yes	—	—	Yes
Footpaths — repair and maintenance, long distance routes, survey, diversion and closure	Yes	Yes	Yes	Yes	Yes	Yes (not long distance routes)	Yes	Yes
HEALTH SERVICES: Local Health Services: (i) Maternity and Child Welfare (ii) Midwives (iii) Health Visitors (iv) Domestic helps (v) Health centres (vi) Vaccination and immunisation (vii) Home Nursing (viii) Prevention of illness	Yes	Yes	(Yes)	(Yes) (where delegated)	(Yes)	—	—	Yes

(ix) Care and after-care of the sick	—	Yes	Yes	Yes	—	Yes (out-country housing)	Yes
(x) Mental Health	Yes	—	—	—	—	—	Yes
Housing, including provision of houses, slum clearance, re-development, over-crowding, improvement grants	Yes	Yes	Yes	Yes	—	—	—
Lodging temporarily homeless people	Yes	—	—	—	—	—	Yes
Housing conditions—supervision in rural areas	—	—	—	—	—	—	—
Housing for employees, provision	—	—	—	—	—	—	—
Housing mortgage advances (under Housing Acts or Small Dwellings Acquisition Acts) and including giving guarantee to Building Societies	Yes	Yes	Yes	Yes	—	—	Yes
Infectious diseases—notification, disinfection and prevention	Yes	Yes	Yes	Yes	—	—	Yes
Information centres	Yes	Yes	Yes	Yes	—	Yes	Yes
Land Acquisition	Yes	Yes	Yes	Yes	—	Yes	Yes
Land charges registration	Yes	Yes	Yes	Yes	—	—	Yes
Land drainage	Yes	—	—	—	—	Yes	Yes
Legal Aid (Legal Aid and Advice Act, 1949)	Yes	—	—	—	Some	Yes	—
Libraries and museums	Yes	Some	Some	Museums only	Libraries only	Museums only	Yes

POWERS AND DUTIES OF LOCAL AUTHORITIES (contd.)

Powers and Duties of Local Authorities	County Councils	County Borough Councils	Non-County Borough Councils	Urban District Councils	Rural District Councils	Parish Councils (Rural)	Greater London Council	London Borough Councils
Licences — dogs, game, guns, hackney carriages and drivers, hawkers, money-lenders, nurses' agencies, pawnbrokers, pet animals, petroleum, milk, slaughterhouses, rag flock, poisons, masseur, hairdressing, employment agencies	Various	Various	Various	Various	Various	—	—	Yes
Life-saving apparatus	—	Yes	Yes	Yes	Yes	—	—	Yes
Litter Act	Yes	Yes	Yes	Yes	Yes	Yes	Yes	Yes
Markets	—	Yes	Yes	Yes	Yes (with consent of Minister)	—	—	Yes
Meat inspection at slaughter-houses	—	Yes	Yes	Yes	Yes	—	—	Yes
Milk inspection	—	Yes	Yes	Yes	Yes	—	—	Yes
Motor vehicles and drivers licensing	Yes	Yes	—	—	—	—	Yes	—
Naming of streets and numbering of houses	—	Yes	Yes	Yes	Yes	—	Naming of streets	Numbering of houses
National Assistance Act: welfare functions	Yes	Yes	Yes	Yes	Yes	—	—	Yes
National Parks — establishment of nature reserves	Yes	—	(where delegated) (county districts can act with the consent of the county council and the Nature Conservancy)			—	—	—

	1	2	3	4	5	6	7
National Parks and Areas of outstanding Natural Beauty	Yes	Yes	—	—	—	—	Yes
Nuisances — suppression of	—	Yes	Yes	Yes	Yes	Yes	Yes
Nurseries and child minders regulation	Yes	Yes	Yes	Yes	Yes	—	Yes
Nursing Homes registration	Yes	Yes	—	—	—	—	Yes
Offensive trades — authorisation and inspection	—	Yes	Yes	Yes	Yes	—	Yes
Offices Act, 1960: Enforcement by L.As. of regulations made by Home Secretary	—	Yes	Yes	Yes	Yes	—	Yes
Oil Burners Act, 1960 — enforcement by L.As. of regulations made by Home Secretary	—	Yes	Yes	Yes	Yes	—	Yes
Omnibus shelters	Yes	Yes	Yes	Yes	Yes	Yes	Yes
Parking Places	Yes (In a National Park or area of outstanding natural beauty)	Yes	—	—	—	Yes	Yes
Parks, Open Spaces, pleasure and recreation grounds	Yes	Yes	Yes Cambridge and Peterborough	Yes	Yes	Yes	—
Physical Training and Recreation Act, 1937, for the provision of gymnasia, camping sites, etc.	Yes	Yes	Yes	Yes	Yes	Yes	Yes
Police (outside Metropolitan Police area)	Yes	Yes	—	—	—	—	—

POWERS AND DUTIES OF LOCAL AUTHORITIES (contd.)

Powers and Duties of Local Authorities	County Councils	County Borough Councils	Non-County Borough Councils	Urban District Councils	Rural District Councils	Parish Councils (Rural)	Greater London Council	London Borough Councils
Pool Betting Act, 1954 — Registration of pools promoters	Yes	Yes	—	—	—	—	Yes	—
Port Health, including action under Aliens Orders, 1920-1953	Yes	Yes	Yes	Yes	Yes	—	Yes	—
Prevention of damage by pests, including rodent control	—	Yes	Yes	Yes	Yes	—	—	Yes
Private Street Works	Yes (in rural areas)	Yes	Yes	Yes	—	—	—	Yes
Protection of Animals, performing	Yes	Yes	—	—	—	—	Yes	—
pets	—	Yes	Yes	Yes	Yes	—	—	Yes
Probation Service	Yes	Some	—	—	—	—	Yes	—
Public Conveniences	—	Yes	Yes	Yes	Yes	—	—	Yes
Public Transport	—	Yes	Yes	—	—	—	—	—
Rates — levying and collection	—	Yes	Yes	Yes	Yes	—	—	Yes
Refuse collection and disposal	—	Yes	Yes	Yes	Yes	—	Disposal only	Yes
Registration of electors	—	Yes	Yes	Yes	Yes	—	Yes	Yes
Remand Homes	Yes	Yes	—	—	—	—	—	Yes
Rent Control (various powers)	—	Yes	Yes	Yes	Yes	—	—	Yes
Reservoirs — safety of	Yes	Yes	—	—	—	—	—	Yes
River Boards, representation on	Yes	Yes	Yes	Yes	Yes	—	—	—
Road Safety	—	Yes	Yes	Yes	Yes	—	—	Yes
Roads:— (i) construction	Yes	Yes	—	—	—	—	Yes	Yes
(ii) maintenance	Yes	Yes	Yes	Yes	—	—	Yes	Yes
(iii) lighting	—	Yes	Yes	Yes	Yes	Yes	Yes	Yes

	C1	C2	C3	C4	C5	C6	C7	C8
Sanitary (Public Health) services	—	Yes	Yes	Yes	Yes	—	—	Yes
Sea Fisheries Act	Yes	Yes	—	—	—	—	—	—
Sewerage and Sewage disposal	—	Yes	Yes	Yes	Yes	—	Yes	Yes
Shops Inspection	Yes	Yes	Yes	Yes	Yes	—	Yes	Yes
Small Lotteries and Gaming Act, 1956	—	Yes	Yes	Yes	Yes	—	—	Yes
Town and Country Planning: 1. Preparation and revision of development plan	Yes	Yes	—	—	—	—	Yes	—
2. Planning control, including advertisement control and the preservation of trees	Yes	Yes	(Yes)	(Yes) (where delegated)	(Yes)	—	—	Yes
Town Development Act, 1952, (powers vary as to whether receiving or disposing of population)	Yes	Yes	Yes	Yes	Yes	—	Yes	Yes
Town Halls, Council Offices, Parish Halls, etc.	Yes	Yes	Yes	Yes	Yes	Yes	Yes	Yes
Vaccination and immunisation	Yes	Yes	—	—	—	—	—	Yes
Valuation, miscellaneous powers	Yes	Yes	Yes	Yes	Yes	—	Yes	Yes
War Memorials — Maintenance	Yes	Yes	Yes	—	—	Yes	—	Yes
Water courses — sanitary control of	—	Yes	Yes	Yes	Yes	Yes	Yes	Yes
Water supply	Anglesey only Yes	Yes	Yes	Yes	Yes	—	—	—
Weights and Measures — inspection	Yes	Yes (if popn. 10,000 or over)	—	—	—	—	—	Yes

POWERS AND DUTIES OF LOCAL AUTHORITIES (contd.)

Powers and Duties of Local Authorities	County Councils	County Borough Councils	Non-County Borough Councils	Urban District Councils	Rural District Councils	Parish Councils (Rural)	Greater London Council	London Borough Councils
Welfare services for aged and handicapped	Yes	Yes	—	—	—	—	—	Yes
Wild Birds Protection Act ..	Yes	Yes	Yes	Yes	Yes	—	Yes	Yes
Youth Employment Service (except where service is operated by Ministry of Labour and National Service)	Yes	Yes	—	—	—	—	Yes Inner London	Yes Outer London

NOTES:

The Common Council of the City of London has similar but not identical, functions to the London Boroughs.

" Inner London " refers to the area of the old L.C.C.

" Outer London " refers to that part of the Greater London area outside the old L.C.C.

This table is based on material supplied by the Ministry of Housing and Local Government. I am most grateful to the Ministry for their assistance.

APPENDIX B

POPULATION OF LOCAL AUTHORITIES

The table below gives a broad picture of the variations in size of local authorities in England and Wales outside the L.C.C. area. The figures refer to 1963. Inevitably, the table must become increasingly out-of-date as the current re-organisation of local government proceeds.

000's	County Councils	County Boroughs	Non-County Boroughs	Urban Districts	Rural Districts
Over 1,000	7	1	—	—	—
500–1,000	11	3	—	—	—
400–500	8	2	—	—	—
300–400	9	3	1	—	—
200–300	5	9	14	2	1
100–200	9	31	7	—	1
90–100	2	3	3	3	1
80–90	2	8	12	3	—
70–80	1	8	14	7	4
60–70	1	8	26	8	14
50–60	3	6	34	16	23
40–50	1	—	34	36	40
30–40	1	1	34	77	93
20–30	1	—	25	70	83
15–20	—	—	29	91	85
10–15	—	—	37	130	90
5–10	—	—	47	121	39
Under 5	—	—	—	—	—
Totals	62	83	317	564	474

APPENDIX C
DEPARTMENTAL LAY-OUT—AVERAGE COUNTY BOROUGH
(say 100,000 to 150,000 population)

Department.	Departmental Head and principal assistants.	Main classes of staff engaged.
Town Clerk.	Town Clerk. Deputy Town Clerk. Senior Assistant solicitor. Chief Administrative Assistant or Chief Committee-clerk.	Solicitors. Committee clerks. Law clerks. Licensing clerks. Registration clerks. General clerks and short-hand-typists.
Treasurer or Accountant.	Treasurer or Accountant. Deputy Treasurer. Chief Accountancy Assistant Chief internal auditor.	Cashiers. Bookkeepers. Rental clerks. Audit clerks. Rate collectors. General clerks. Shorthand-typists.
Public Health.	Medical Officer of Health. Deputy or assistant medical officer. Chief Public Health Inspector. Administrative Assistant or Chief Clerk.	Clinical and school medical officers. Public Health Inspectors. Health Visitors. Nurses. Laboratory assistants. Clerks, typists, etc.
Education.	Chief Education Officer. Deputy Education Officer. Inspector of schools.	Administrative assistants. Clerks. Attendance and welfare officers. Shorthand-typists.
Engineer and Surveyor.	Engineer and Surveyor. Deputy. Chief Engineering assistant. Chief Architectural assistant. Housing Manager. Sewage Works Manager. Chief Administrative Assistant or Chief Clerk. *There may be separate Architect's and/or Housing Management Departments.*	Highway surveyors. Building surveyors. Assistant Civil Engineers. Architects. Town Planning assistants. Sewage Works chemists or assistants. Mechanical engineering assistants. Administrative and general assistants. Clerks. Tracers. Shorthand-typists.
Police.	Chief Constable. Superintendent.	Inspectors. Sergeants. Constables. Clerks and typists.
Fire.	Chief Fire Brigade Officer. Assistant or Deputy.	Fire Brigade Officers. Clerks, etc.

Department.	Departmental Head and principal assistants.	Main classes of staff engaged.
Welfare, etc.	Arrangements flexible under National Health Act, 1946, National Assistance Act, 1948, and Children Act, 1948.*	
Cleansing & Lighting.	Superintendent.	Clerks. Shorthand-typists.
Libraries.	Librarian. Deputy.	Assistant Librarians. Clerks. Shorthand-typists.
Museums & Art Galleries.	Curator.	Assistants.
Water.	Engineer and Manager. Deputy.	Mechanical Engineers. Administrative assistants & clerks. Shorthand-typists.
Transport.	General Manager. Deputy.	Mechanical Engineers. Traffic superintendent. Administrative assistants & clerks. Statistical clerks. Inspectors. Cashiers. Shorthand-typists.
Parks and Cemeteries.	Superintendent.	Clerks. Typists.
Weights and Measures.	Chief Inspector.	Assistant Inspectors. Clerks and Typists.
Markets.	Superintendent.	Inspectors. Assistants. Clerks. Shorthand-typists.
Baths.	Superintendent.	Clerks, etc.

*Chief Welfare Officers are appointed by some Authorities but other officers e.g. Chief Education Officers, Medical Officers of Health, Children Officers, are affected by the functions.

Index

For Product Safety Concerns and Information please contact our EU
representative GPSR@taylorandfrancis.com
Taylor & Francis Verlag GmbH, Kaufingerstraße 24, 80331 München, Germany

* 9 7 8 1 0 3 2 9 0 2 9 3 7 *